MICHIGAN INTERNATIONAL BUSINESS STUDIES
Number 18

# ECONOMIC POLICIES IN FRANCE 1976-1981

The Barre Program in a West European Perspective

## W. ALLEN SPIVEY

Michigan International Business Studies No. 18
Division of Research
Graduate School of Business Administration
The University of Michigan
Ann Arbor

338.944
S761e

Copyright © 1982
by The University of Michigan

**Library of Congress Cataloging in Publication Data**

Spivey, W. Allen.
    Economic policies in France, 1976-81.

    (Michigan international business studies ; no. 18)

    Includes bibliographical references.
    1. France – Economic policy – 1945-      I. Title.
II. Series.
HC276.2.S65   1982          338.944          82-12077
ISBN 0-87712-223-7

83-3711

# Contents

# Preface

This is a brief study of major aspects of the economic policies developed in France under Raymond Barre when he was prime minister from August 1976 until May 1981. These policies, often referred to as the Barre program, naturally have both supporters and opponents. The program's emphasis on freeing markets, discarding price controls, encouraging French firms to become more competitive in international markets, and stabilizing the franc appealed to economists and others in France and elsewhere and, notably, to the Western financial press. At the same time this program aroused the ire of members of the Left.

A variety of important influences – the restrained and even surgical application of demand management policies; the increasing severity of the French unemployment problem which was, and continues to be, closely related to the rapid growth of the labor force and population; the continuing difficulties of France's financial system and international trade position; and, finally, the second oil shock – all came together in late 1979 and 1980 to cause formidable difficulties for M. Barre and for the then president, Giscard d'Estaing. The increasing unemployment and, it has been asserted, the growing personal unpopularity of Giscard were principal components in the latter's loss to the Socialists in the elections of April and May 1981, thus bringing the Barre program to an end at a time when some important and favorable underlying changes in the French economy were beginning to solidify.

In dealing with this tapestry of events – largely from an economic point of view – I have repeatedly attempted two things: to sketch a brief historical background for the problem considered and to place my assessment of the French situation in a context of similar developments in other western European nations and, often, in the United States and Japan as well. Because the new Socialist government quickly proceeded to overturn many of the Barre policies as I was completing this work, I decided to include a final chapter on its performance during its first seven or eight months in power and so provide still another context within which to view the Barre program. In this chapter I also venture to make some largely nonquantitative forecasts, the somber nature of which readers can evaluate for themselves.

vii

A study of this kind necessarily draws on the work of many others and I owe a considerable debt to a large number of persons whom I have attempted to acknowledge through ample, but I hope not excessive, footnotes. I have also placed notes at the end of each of the first three chapters indicating additional sources of information available in both French and English. I am grateful for the help extended to me by members of M. Barre's administration in the course of often frank conversations and by colleagues at French and American universities. I refrain from acknowledging them by name for fear that any list will surely omit at least several persons who provided me with assistance. The Olin Foundation supported part of my work and writing and made a travel grant available to me.

Finally, I wish to acknowledge the help I received from a different quarter: from conversations with neighbors in our apartment building in Paris, from the landlady herself, from persons I came to know in nearby shops owned by *petits commerçants* (who never failed to speak to me when I encountered them on the street and outside their working habitats), and other friends in France. They seemed always ready to respond to my questions on politics, life in France, and related subjects with that volubility, flair, and diverse individuality which I came to admire and even to be fond of, and deepened my appreciation of Michelet's interesting expression: *La France est une personne.*

W. ALLEN SPIVEY

*February 1982*

# 1

# Background

## Some Economic Developments in Outline, 1946-73

France emerged from over five years of occupation during World War II with a disrupted economy and a depleted capital base. Rebuilding began in early 1946 and progressed throughout the Fourth Republic, but political uncertainties – France had 15 cabinets between 1947 and 1954 – persistent balance of payments problems, and continuing inflation served to restrain progress.[1] By 1958, when the Fifth Republic was launched and France joined the European Economic Community (EEC), economic progress had begun to accelerate. This was subsequently aided by the monetary stabilization facilitated by the policies of Pinay and Rueff. Modernization of industry progressed more rapidly; there was less protectionism in foreign trade, which can be attributed in part to EEC participation and associated arrangements; exports experienced healthy increases; and real income made important gains. This progress continued throughout the 1960s. Even the disruptions following the "events" of May and June 1968 (les événements) seemed to be quickly alleviated, and France's economic expansion resumed the brisk pace characteristic of the decade as a whole. France's annual rates of growth in real Gross Domestic Product (GDP) were either at the top or near it among EEC countries during the period 1958-73.

## The End of the Banquet Years, 1974-76

The international commodity crisis, the oil embargo of 1973-74, and the sharp rises in energy prices struck France more severely than some, perhaps most, of the other principal industrial nations of the West, inaugurating a period of much slower economic growth in France. Moreover, the quadrupling of oil prices had a major impact on the French economy because France at that time was importing approximately 75 percent of her primary energy supplies. This can be

1. It is conventional to delineate periods in French history in governmental terms. The following chronology is a standard one: First Republic, 1792-99; Second Republic, 1848-52; Third Republic, 1870-1940; Fourth Republic, 1944-58; Fifth Republic, 1958-present.

contrasted with an EEC average of 55 percent and with the 38 percent that France had imported in the year 1960. In 1973 France was the third largest importer of oil (after Japan and the U.S.) and the third largest importer of natural gas (after the U.S. and West Germany).[2] One economist has estimated that the impact of rising energy prices was equivalent to a 3 percent tax on the country's national income.[3]

The policy response to the changed energy supply situation and to the international adjustments that it set off was initially sluggish. The expansionary economic policies of the previous 10 years were largely continued until the middle of 1974, perhaps because of the presidential elections held in May of that year. (In the second-round election between Giscard d'Estaing and Mitterand, the former won by a hair, 50.6 percent to 49.4 percent; Jacques Chirac was named prime minister.) The economic repercussions of the oil crisis and the sluggish policy response soon combined to generate adverse consequences in France. Imports grew at a rate exceeding that of Gross Domestic Product, the rate of increase in consumer prices accelerated, hourly wage rates increased about 20 percent in the year ending in the third quarter of 1974, and real weekly earnings rose about 3 percent in the same period, while at the same time there was a decrease in the average number of hours worked. Moreover, energy prices in France, largely controlled by the government, did not rise commensurately with the rise in the world market price of oil.

Following the May 1974 elections, an antiinflationary policy had been put into place by the fall of that year. Some additional taxes were to be imposed; government expenditures, particularly those relating to public investments, were to be moderated; and the current account deficit was to be reduced. Although there were differences between intentions and actions, increases in consumer prices were softened and there was an improvement in France's balance of payments; but a fall in domestic industrial production also occurred. Profit margins likewise fell during this period, the number of business failures increased by about 60 percent from mid-1973 to mid-1975, and real or constant franc GDP declined from its third-quarter 1973 level in each subsequent quarter until the fourth quarter of 1975. Despite this, however, consumption and real weekly earnings rose over the same period, fueled by an increase in the minimum wage or SMIC (*salaire minimum interprofessionel de croissance*), which

2. G. de Carmoy, "French Energy Policy," a paper prepared for the Conference on the Political Economy of France, American Enterprise Institute for Public Policy Research, Washington, D.C., May 29–31, 1980.

3. B. Belassa, "L'Economie française sous la cinquième république 1958–1978," *Revue économique* 30 (1979):955.

rose at an average annual rate of 19.4 percent from 1973 to 1975. This rate was well above the rate of increase in wage rates in manufacturing and in the consumer price index (CPI), although the initial minimum wage levels were low relative to the average of EEC countries.

By the fall of 1975 another sequence of expansionary policies, which included tax benefits for private investments and some adjustments in business taxes, was deemed necessary. These policies contributed to the rises in real GDP and industrial production that occurred in the fall of 1975, but these quickly spilled over into increased consumption which, combined with the increase in domestic real money wages, contributed to a deterioration in France's balance of payments (a deficit in the current account balance being one result). The franc declined against currencies of importance to France and this, together with a rise in labor costs, led to another round of unfavorable influences on profit margins and industrial production by the middle of 1976.

Thus an initially sluggish policy response was followed by a sequence of "stop and go" policies—or, perhaps more accurately, "go and stop" policies. Moreover, because these policies had different impacts on wages and consumption than on profit margins and industrial output, France was one of the few countries of the industrialized world in which the results of the oil crisis of 1973–74 were largely paid for out of the profits of private enterprise.[4] Also, average hourly wage rates grew by 17 percent in 1975 and by about 15 percent in 1976, while productivity declined during the same period and the inflation rate varied between 10 and 12 percent.

As will be seen at various points in this study, many of France's problems and challenges arise from its mixed economy and its middle power status. France does not have the economic and strategic power of a country such as the U.S., and the franc is sensitive to interactions between domestic economic policies and forces at work in the world economy, particularly trade with West Germany; so policymaking across a broad range of issues must address extremely difficult "trade-off" questions.[5] Moreover, the continuing inclination of the govern-

4. A Fourçans, "Has Monsieur Barre's Experiment in Monetarism Failed?," the Paris Lecture given at the City University of London, May 13, 1980, p. 5; Belassa, pp. 960–71.

5. Neither the current magnitude nor the steadily growing importance of foreign trade in the French economy is fully appreciated. The ratio of French exports to GDP is often cited as a measure of the importance of foreign trade; but the ratio of exports to the production of goods is a more informative figure because GDP includes expenditures on services, most of which are not involved in international transactions, whereas services are excluded from the latter. These ratios for selected years are (in terms of current prices):

ment's large administrative apparatus towards *dirigisme* and selective but sustained and well-organized intervention also leads, as will be seen throughout this study, to a variety of domestic economic problems which have important repercussions on France's international activities. These influences and problems are reflected in France's monetary-fiscal–foreign exchange policy mix, and even a brief discussion of the 1973–75 period must include some consideration of this mix and the problems that France experienced with it.

First of all, the money supply grew relatively rapidly throughout the period, and reserve ratios and interest rates also increased (there was some softening in the latter by the last quarter of 1974). Table 1 shows percent changes in M2 (*masse monétaire*) during the four-quarter periods ending in the quarters indicated (for example, 14.74 is the percent change in M2 from the first quarter of 1972 through the first quarter of 1973).[6]

Money stock growth rates rose to high levels, particularly during the period 1975.2 through 1976.2; beginning with the fourth quarter of 1976, however, there was a significant drop in the rate of increase (we will return to a discussion of this in the fourth section of Chapter 3, which is concerned with monetary policy). At the same time that money supply and real weekly earnings were growing, additional price controls were being actively applied, largely by means of a collection of contractual agreements with firms which allowed for fixed average rates of increase in industrial prices and for some "pass-through" of changes in costs of materials and of specified energy inputs.[7] At the end of 1974, and against the vigorous opposition of business, a complex system of controls called the provisional levy was introduced by the government. This provided for a refundable tax on increases in profit margins which was, supposedly, to have the

|  | 1970 | 1975 | 1976 | 1977 | 1978 | 1979 | 1980 |
|---|---|---|---|---|---|---|---|
| Ratio of Exports to GDP | 12.8 | 15.4 | 15.8 | 16.5 | 16.0 | 17.0 | 17.8 |
| Ratio of Exports to Production of Goods | 30.6 | 46.2 | 48.1 | 50.1 | 49.6 | 52.2 | 54.6 |

From *International Economic Indicators* (Washington, D.C.: U.S. Department of Commerce, September 1981), p. 36.

6. M2 includes coins and notes in circulation outside the Banque de France; current accounts at the Banque de France, the Treasury, and the post office; time, demand, and savings deposits; certificates of deposit; and time deposits at the Treasury. For details of French money supply variables and those of other major nations, see R. C. Bryant, *Money and Monetary Policy in Interdependent Nations* (Washington, D.C.: The Brookings Institution, 1980), chap. 3.

7. This discussion draws extensively on the excellent treatment of monetary and fiscal policy trade-offs and their impact on exchange rates in five countries to be found in S. W. Black, *Floating Exchange Rates and National Economic Policy* (New Haven: Yale University Press, 1977).

TABLE 1

Percent Increase in M2, France

| Quarter | Percent |
|---------|---------|
| 1973.1  | 14.74   |
| .2      | 13.78   |
| .3      | 13.04   |
| .4      | 14.86   |
| 1974.1  | 17.40   |
| .2      | 15.21   |
| .3      | 15.30   |
| .4      | 15.86   |
| 1975.1  | 15.42   |
| .2      | 16.32   |
| .3      | 17.67   |
| .4      | 18.14   |
| 1976.1  | 18.65   |
| .2      | 18.94   |
| .3      | 16.00   |
| .4      | 12.81   |
| 1977.1  | 12.42   |
| .2      | 10.55   |
| .3      | 12.89   |
| .4      | 13.92   |

*Source:* Data supplied by Institut national de la statistique et des études économiques (INSEE), Paris. M2 quarterly data from which percent changes are calculated are for the last month of the given quarter, seasonally adjusted.

result of holding the levels of these margins down. This system was suspended in the following year, largely because the recession of 1975 made it unnecessary.[8]

Because of the increase in energy prices and the incompatibility of French and West German economic policies, the franc was forced out of the snake currency agreement (see below) in January 1974. The franc then depreciated about 6 percent against the mark and prices of imports from West Germany rose, exerting increased inflationary pressures on the domestic economy.

It may be helpful to give a brief review of the snake currency agreement and some of the issues relating to it. Currency agreements have a long history and have been an important if frustrating part of international monetary relations since the Bretton Woods conference in 1943. There have been many meetings and lengthy deliberations over the years as countries have struggled to reconcile domestic economic policies and movements in foreign exchange rates. Many policies have been advocated and controverted: pegged exchange rates,

8. Ibid., pp. 89–90.

adjustable-peg systems (such a system was in effect among most non-Communist governments from 1946 until 1971), floating systems, and managed floating systems (sometimes called "dirty floating," in which exchange rates are allowed to float but are "nudged" in various ways, either frequently or infrequently, by governments). The subtle variants and details of these policies cannot be considered here, but the interested reader can consult the notes at the end of this chapter for suggestions for further reading.

In the early 1970s seven European nations (Belgium, France, West Germany, Italy, Luxembourg, the Netherlands, and Great Britain) attempted to move toward a common European currency by means of a "narrow-margins agreement" which obligated each country's central bank to maintain a narrow range of variation for selected intra-European exchange rates. If one currency became very strong relative to another, for example, the central banks involved were required to take action even though both the currencies were within the permissible band in terms of their dollar parity. Interventions of this kind were supposed to keep the dollar price of these currencies very close to each other, gradually narrowing the permissible variation in these rates to zero. Exchange rates between these countries would then become essentially fixed and there would be a "common money" between them. This agreement, implemented in 1972, was called the "snake in the tunnel." As the permissible variation in the exchange rates of participating countries approached zero, the snake would grow thinner and thinner, disappearing altogether when the rates converged into a "common value." Various countries in addition to France left the snake for different periods of time (Britain left it after two months and did not return). The tunnel became essentially irrelevant after about a year as economic policies, money growth, and inflation rates in participating countries diverged, causing exchange rates to diverge also.

Despite the failure of the snake and of many other similar agreements, the concept of European monetary unification – or more generally, of regional currency blocks – is far from dead. A new organization, the European Monetary System, was established in March 1979 to encourage former members of the snake to cooperate in reducing intra-European exchange rate variation.[9] Converging exchange rates are seen as an ideal for the European community, particularly by

9. Currency agreements and their principal economic features are described in introductory international economic texts. An excellent source is J. D. Richardson, *Understanding International Economics: Theory and Practice* (Boston: Little, Brown and Co., 1980), chap. 7, on which this discussion draws. See also C. Allsopp, "The Political Economy of E.M.S.," *Revue économique* 30 (1979):866–94; and "The European Monetary System, Structure and Operations," *Monthly Report of the Deutsche Bundesbank* 31 (March 1981):11–18.

some officials in the French government, although it remains a mystery why it should be expected that administrative arrangements and agreements between governments can restrain exchange rates to a narrow band arbitrarily determined through committee negotiation when inflation rates diverge markedly and when the domestic economic policies of participating governments are "not coordinated."[10] There is wide agreement among economists of vastly different value positions that exchange rates cannot be independently managed against market forces. In any case, attempts to establish fixed exchange rates with respect to West Germany would have severe implications, because continuing problems of inflation in France produce higher domestic inflation rates than in West Germany and consistently tend to erode the competitiveness of French industries vis-à-vis those in West Germany.

Returning to a discussion of France in 1974: when Giscard d'Estaing became president in June of that year, the goal of establishing a strong franc was apparently adopted. The franc appreciated against the mark, moving towards its former parity level with that currency; and aided by a declining value in the U.S. dollar, extensive foreign borrowing, and associated improvement in the trade balance, the franc rose sufficiently relative to the mark so that it was able to rejoin the snake in July 1975. However, as noted above, a reviving economy again put the franc under pressure on the foreign exchanges. Conflicts were generated by differing inflation rates in France and other European countries, notably West Germany; these led to enormous difficulties for those attempting to peg exchange rates between these countries, and the ensuing speculative movements on the foreign exchanges cost France an estimated 23 billion francs of reserves in the first quarter of 1976. As a result, France had to leave the snake a second time in March of that year.

To summarize, France decided to join the snake in 1972 and to peg

10. The following is a partial commentary on the quoted words. Many knowledgeable observers have stressed that proper coordination of domestic economic policies to achieve and maintain international exchange rate policies is impossible ("political leaders are not reputed to have a natural inclination to sacrifice themselves for the voters of another country," as H. B. Malmgren has noted in "Interaction of Financial and Commercial Markets: Challenge for Policy Makers," *The World Economy* 3 [1980]:288]. Concerning the importance of the expectations of economic agents in exchange rate determination, Malmgren also says: "Motivations based on considerations of the comparative price and yield of an asset in different currencies may overwhelm motivations derived from transactions, in which case the primary determinants of exchange rates are expectations about future values and yields. These expectations may be partly based on the recent current-account balance experience of a country, but they will also reflect expectations about inflation, productivity, political safety, national politics and economic policies—especially monetary (interest-rate) policy. As with equity markets, expectations are also conditioned by what other buyers and sellers [of financial assets] expect." (pp. 292–93)

the franc to the value of the deutsche mark. However, France was subsequently unable to maintain as low a domestic inflation rate as West Germany, largely because wage rates could not be restrained to noninflationary levels. Because trade with West Germany was important to France (about 20 percent of her imports came from West Germany in 1975 and about the same percentage of her exports went to this country), France experienced a deteriorating competitive position over most of the period 1971–75.

Moreover, owing to the delay caused by the elections of 1974, French fiscal policy became contractionary just as economic conditions in France were moving into a recessionary phase. Thus, fiscal policy was "procyclical" at this time rather than countercyclical.[11] On the other hand, money stock (see Table 1) was growing rapidly, and at the same time France was taking actions to appreciate the franc against the deutsche mark. The policy mix lacked coherence, and important elements of it appeared either to be in opposition to each other, or to have been developed and implemented with inadequate appreciation of the inevitable interrelations between them. When it is recalled that both monetary and fiscal policies express themselves with lags of five or six quarters or more, and that additional time is required, once a new policy takes hold, before it affects relative prices and then investment, the mix may well have had a destabilizing effect on the economy. A recent macroeconomic study investigated alternate investment functions in France and West Germany since 1973 and presented parallel simulations for each country in order to analyze the effects of fiscal and monetary policies on investment.[12] The actual policies of each country were compared with neutral policies which involved no attempt to counteract major economic fluctuations. The study concluded that although neutral policies would have failed to avoid recession in either country, the policies actually followed aggravated the cyclical-type downturns that were experienced and were destabilizing in their effects. In any case, the effects of these policies, together with the large shifts in real energy costs and rises in real wages, put great pressure on French industry, which was also hemmed in at the time by price controls and other restraints. An example of the latter was an aspect of the government's reaction to energy problems in 1974; according to de Carmoy, "French industry was sacrificed to the road as the price of

11. Black, p. 129. Important features of the economic policies of the period 1974 to mid-1976 are sometimes associated with J.-P. Fourcade, who was finance minister at the time.
12. P. Artus, P.-A. Muet, P. Palinkas, and P. Pauly, "Economic Policy and Private Investment since the Oil Crisis: A Comparative Study of France and Germany," *European Economic Review* 16 (1981):7–51.

industrial fuel was increased by 91 percent and the price of gasoline by 29 percent."[13] The economic policy record for 1974–76 was a poor one, and a new orientation was clearly needed. This came about two years after the election of Giscard d'Estaing as president with the appointment of Raymond Barre as prime minister. The program of the latter is the subject of the remainder of this study.

## Notes on Chapter 1

Because only a highly condensed summary of many complex events is given here and because references on economic matters in France are often elusive to many English-speaking readers, additional sources of information beyond those cited may be useful. A general historical account of the period 1944 through 1962 can be found in A. Cobban's *A History of Modern France,* volume 3 (London: Penguin Books, 1965). Volumes 1 and 2 are also standard references; volume 1 goes back to 1715. A lucidly written study of French history from 1750 is available in one volume: G. Wright's *France in Modern Times,* 3rd edition (New York: W. W. Norton and Co., 1981).

A readable, brief discussion of the political forces, political structures, and French experiences since 1945 is found in Chapters 1 through 4 of *Contemporary France, Politics and Society since 1945,* by D. L. Hanley, A. P. Kerr, and N. H. Waites (London: Routledge & Kegan Paul, 1979). This book also provides a good, brief statement of the politics of the 1974–76 period and of events leading to the appointment of M. Barre as prime minister. The papers in *The Fifth Republic at Twenty,* edited by W. G. Andrews and S. Hoffmann (Albany: State University of New York Press, 1981), provide a good survey of governmental, political, and economic aspects of the Fifth Republic. A well-written study emphasizing political features and processes is J. E. S. Hayward's book, *The One and Indivisible French Republic* (London: Weidenfeld and Nicholson, 1973). This is by now (inevitably) dated, and some of its generalizations must be revised in the light of subsequent developments. A lively account of contemporary France and of its major institutions and other features is J. Ardagh's *The New France,* 3rd edition (London: Penguin Books, 1977). This book races along at such a fast pace that complex issues often receive excessively superficial consideration; it is nonetheless what the British call a jolly good read.

*Economie et statistique,* a monthly publication of the Institut national

13. De Carmoy, p. 7.

de la statistique et des études économiques (INSEE), is an excellent source of information. The following articles, all from this publication, are important references. C. Sautter deals with productivity, profits, and employment from 1954–74 in "L'Efficacité et la rentabilité de l'économie française de 1954 à 1974," 68 (June 1975):7–21, and in "Investissement et emploi dans une hypothèse de croissance ralentie," 93 (October 1977):3–20. Investment, credit, and business failures are studied in J. Albert and L. Vialet's "Les Défaillances d'entreprises depuis dix ans: un tournant en 1974," 95 (December 1977):5–41. R. Boyer and P. Petit examine employment and productivity in France and the EEC countries between 1960 and 1977 in "Emploi et productivité dans la CEE," 121 (April-May 1980):35–59. Comparisons of real GDP and purchasing power indices for European and other countries are treated in H. Picard's "Les Régions selon leur PIB en valeur réele," 111 (May 1979):47–64.

The problem of exchange rates and their relation to domestic monetary and fiscal policies is a complex and tortuous one. The various international agreements that have been devoted to problems of exchange rate management and related issues are treated in introductory textbooks in international economics. An excellent study going beyond these is J. D. Murphy's *The International Monetary System* (Washington: The American Enterprise Institute for Public Policy Research, 1979), particularly Chapters 1, 3, 4, 5, and 9. The politics of international economic relations, including the Bretton Woods agreement, the establishment of the International Monetary Fund and other such agencies, as well as the background of the multilateralism movement extending from the aftermath of World War II, are discussed by R. N. Gardner in *Sterling-Dollar Diplomacy in Current Perspective* (New York: Columbia University Press, 1980).

Various aspects of exchange rates and their relation to domestic economic policy are treated in *The Economics of Exchange Rates,* edited by J. A. Frenkel and H. G. Johnson (Reading, Mass.: Addison-Wesley Publishing Co., 1978). A case for managed floating of exchange rates is made by R. C. Bryant in *Financial Interdependence and Variability in Exchange Rates* (Washington: The Brookings Institution, 1980). A good survey of the principal points of view on exchange rate adjustment is M. Wolff's "Tower of Babel, Conflicting Ideologies of Adjustment," *The World Economy* 4 (February 1980):481–96. J. H. Makin explores how monetary and other economic policies influence exchange rates whether they are fixed or floating in "Fixed versus Floating: A Red Herring," *Columbia Journal of World Business* (Winter 1979):7–14. G. Haberler is the author of two scholarly overviews: "The Dollar in the World Economy: Recent Developments in Perspec-

tive," in *Contemporary Economic Problems 1980,* edited by W. Feller
(Washington: The American Enterprise Institute for Public Policy
Research, 1980):135–68; and "Flexible Exchange-Rate Theories and
Controversies Once Again," in *Flexible Exchange Rates and the Balance
of Payments: Essays in Memory of Egon Sohmen,* edited by J. S.
Chipman and C. P. Kindleberger (Amsterdam: North-Holland Pub-
lishing Co., 1980). A relatively advanced treatment of theoretical
issues is R. Dornbusch's *Open Economy Macroeconomics* (New York:
Basic Books, 1980).

Two themes appear frequently in contemporary French policy commentary: structural problems and crisis, or *la crise.* The former is an
elastic category; it can include virtually any important political,
economic, social, or organizational problem which appears to be
insoluble except through a far-reaching change deemed by the writer
to be impossible to realize in the short or medium term. Agriculture is
a structural problem; the financial system with its layers of complex
organizations, some of which are outmoded, is a structural problem;
the *grandes écoles* and their influence on the *élites* are structural problems; the stagnation of investment and the continuing gap in new
investment growth in France relative to other Western European
nations constitute a structural problem; and so on. The crisis theme
has a similar portmanteau quality; clearly one man's crisis is another's
structural problem. A book which employs the theme of structural
problems (among others) is *La Grande menace industrielle,* by Chris-
tian Stoffaes (Paris: Calmann-Lévy, 1978). An interesting book
written in a sweeping style, it sometimes verges on the apocalyptic,
as may be intimated by its title. The crisis motif is employed throughout in J. H. Lorenzi, O. Pastré, and J. Toledano's *La Crise du XX$^e$ siècle*
(Paris: Economica, 1980).

# 2

# Aspects of the Barre Program

## The Goals of the Barre Program

Against the background of sharp ups and downs, economic policy shifts, and conflicts between domestic and international policies, Raymond Barre became prime minister of France in August 1976. An economist with a distinguished academic career as well as considerable experience in government and international economic organizations, Barre brought major changes to the economic policies of France. In sharp contrast to many of his predecessors, Barre gave more weight to longer-term considerations in the formation of economic policy. Shortly after taking office he announced a variety of goals: to maintain money supply growth below that of nominal or current franc GDP, to contain budget deficits so that they could be financed without creating money for this purpose, to avoid excessive growth in social expenditures, to eliminate useless regulation of business, to provide incentives for increased investment in the private sector, and to continue to reject pressures for expanding protectionist measures. Barre stressed the importance of balance of payments constraints in the formation of domestic economic policy, and he wanted to achieve greater stability for the franc, particularly with respect to the deutsche mark and the U.S. dollar, by correcting the pronounced deterioration that had taken place in the current account balance and by making related moves to strengthen France's international reserve position.

## Freeing Prices and Accelerating the Return to Markets

Perhaps the most important feature of the Barre program, particularly for the longer term, was the gradual liberalization of domestic prices which began in 1978. This reflected the desire of the government to rely to a much greater extent than previous governments on the operation of market forces (although a return to markets had begun in the 1960s).

The government first decontrolled all producer prices, with the exception of pharmaceuticals refundable under social security coverage and petroleum products. The former system for control of price

13

markups at the distribution stage was also relaxed for industrial prices and for food products, but the prices of private services continued to be subject to negotiations between the government and representatives of the trade or service activity concerned. In 1979 service prices and various other markup restrictions were relaxed in cases when measures to increase competition were agreed upon with the government, and in 1980 most service prices and distributional markups were removed from controls. Various retail price controls were lifted, and in 1980 controls on petroleum product prices were also ended.

There had been many complaints about the price control system, which had been in existence since the end of World War II. The PATRONAT, an association of businessmen from large enterprises, had claimed that it was the most onerous in Western Europe. It also asserted that the system squeezed profit margins; discouraged stockholder investment, and thus perpetuated the unfavorable debt-equity ratios of French businesses relative to those in other Western nations; and encouraged investment outside France (where price controls could not be applied). The PATRONAT also argued that the system was arbitrarily administered by bureaucrats lacking business experience who enjoyed much latitude in interpreting the regulations and who were not accountable for the results of their actions. It was also asserted that business was influenced more by the discipline of bureaucrats than by the discipline of the marketplace. An estimated 30,000 price decrees were issued from this system between 1948 and 1978. A university study estimated that price controls in the steel industry alone had resulted in a cumulative total of 12.9 billion francs of lost profits between 1949 and 1976.

The government also attempted to reduce its subsidies to various industries and to lessen the protection extended to various industry groups which had been sheltered for many years. In contrast to previous policy, some unprofitable firms (openly called lame ducks) were allowed to go bankrupt, others which were in or near bankruptcy (the Boussac textile firm and the Rhône-Poulenc chemical combine were the most notable examples) were not "bailed out" of their difficulties, and some firms whose prospects for returning to profitable operations appeared to be favorable were allowed to close obsolete plants and to reduce their work forces, despite the political unpopularity of these decisions.

These policies produced a variety of favorable results. The current account balance was improved nearly US$ 10 billion between 1976 and 1978; French manufacturing registered productivity gains averaging about 5 percent per year from 1977 through 1979; corporate profits grew about 13 percent in 1978 and slightly more than this in 1979; business investment in plant and equipment rose by 2.7 percent and 3.7 percent, respectively, in these two years; and French businesses were able to finance 77 percent of their investment internally in 1979, in contrast to 61 percent in 1976.

The acceleration in the return to markets was a mixed bag, however, despite the pro-private-enterprise commentary of the government. At the same time that selected lame ducks were being abandoned to drift with the economic current and the influence of the planners in the Commissariat du plan was being reduced even further, there was an increase in some types of selective interventions through the redefined Ministry of Industry, which rapidly made use of France's substantial array of measures related to tax relief, subsidy, credit allocation, procurement, and merger promotion. These were aimed not only at sectors within the economy but also across sectors in geographical regions and even occasionally at individual firms. Many of the moves were designed to encourage what have been called high-technology industries and improve France's competitive position in international markets. These issues will be examined in greater detail in the section of this chapter which addresses the industrial policies of France.

## Energy Problems and Policies

Since 1976 the government has sought to utilize its highly centralized state control of energy affairs to integrate its energy policies more satisfactorily into its economic policy framework. Economy in  the consumption of energy was encouraged by increases in the prices of gasoline, fuel oil, and public transportation. Political problems of timing, largely related to the 1978 Assembly elections, caused increases in these prices to be delayed and then to be "bunched" at various times, with consequent inconveniences to producers and consumers and consequent "lumping" effects in the CPI statistics. The latter thus understated and then overstated underlying price increases. Inflation expectations may also have been adversely influenced by these bunching effects. At the same time, government investment in nuclear energy rose rapidly, and research and development in energy-producing activities (including disposal of nuclear wastes through vitrification processes) was escalated. An examination of various statistics and government reports indicates that the broad goals of energy policy were to achieve a sharp reduction of oil imports, a small increase in coal imports, and a relatively large increase in imports of natural gas, while employing a significant increase in nuclear-generated electricity as the major balancing factor in the aggregate energy demand and supply situation.[1] Table 2 compares France's energy demand and supply situation in 1973 with that projected for the year 1985 (the projections were

TABLE 2

Major Features of France's Energy Demand and Supply
(In millions of tons of oil equivalent)

| Source | Actual, 1973 | Projected, 1985 |
|---|---|---|
| *Consumption* | | |
| Coal | 30.5 | 29.0 |
| Oil | 116.3 | 101.0 |
| Gas | 15.0 | 36.0 |
| Nuclear | 3.0 | 43.0 |
| Hydroelectric | 9.8 | 14.0 |
| New energy sources | 2.0 | 2.0 |
| Total | 176.6 | 225.0 |
| *Production* | | |
| Coal | 18.1 | 10.0 |
| Oil | 2.0 | 3.0 |
| Gas | 6.9 | 5.0 |
| Nuclear | 2.6 | 43.0 |
| Hydroelectric | 10.5 | 14.0 |
| New energy sources | 2.0 | 6.0 |
| Total | 42.1 | 81.0 |
| *New Imports* | | |
| Coal | 11.1 | 20.5 |
| Oil | 114.4 | 93.0 |
| Gas | 8.0 | 30.5 |
| Total | 133.5 | 144.0 |
| *External Dependence* | | |
| Percent | 75.6 | 64.0 |

*Source:* Ministère de l'industrie, *Les chiffres clés de l'énergie* (Paris: 1979); cited in G. de Carmoy, "French Energy Policy," a paper prepared for the Conference on the Political Economy of France, American Enterprise Institute for Public Policy Research, Washington, D.C., May 29–31, 1980, Table 1, p. 2.

1. An assessment of the technical features of the French energy program is outside the scope of this study. Such an assessment would require an examination of such matters as "light water" and "breeder" nuclear reactors, production cost projections and comparisons with anticipated alternate sources and costs of energy, as well as political considerations extending to France's military program and the *force de frappe*. At least one authority has asserted that the true costs of the French nuclear program remain substantially unknown even to the authorities and experts most deeply involved; see the provocative discussion in S. S. Cohen, "Informed Bewilderment: French Economic Strategy and the Crisis," *La Revue Tocqueville* 3 (1980–81):78–113.

developed in 1979). The critical importance of nuclear energy for both future consumption and production is readily apparent from the enormous increases planned, while a 13 percent decrease in domestic consumption of oil and a decrease of nearly 20 percent in net imports of oil are anticipated. France also expects to supply more than half her electricity demand from nuclear sources by 1985. This is an enormous shift in the energy balance sheet of the country, and one wonders what the total investment requirements will turn out to be, and whether in fact this shift can be realized (even if the projected 4 percent per year GDP growth that has been assumed were to occur – a level which seems highly unlikely at this writing). Moreover, despite the magnitude of this shift and the complexity and expense of the technological, managerial, and investment developments associated with it, France's external dependence measure is expected to decrease by only slightly more than 10 percentage points – from about 75 percent to about 64 percent – during this period. While this is a relatively important reduction, France's energy dependence in 1985, even if all goes as planned, will still be great. The magnitude of this dependency is suggested by noting that France's projected 1985 dependence measure of 64 percent is very much larger than it was in 1960 (when it is estimated to have been about 38 percent).

An important feature of France's energy policies is the government's activity in attempting to manage and finance the energy-related balance of payments deficits. A discussion of this matter will be taken up in the sixth section of Chapter 3, which deals with balance of payments policies and which draws on the discussions of monetary and fiscal policies which immediately precede it.

## Employment Problems and Policies

Developments with respect to employment and unemployment have been disappointing. Total civilian employment grew only about 1 percent from 1975 to 1979. Although service employment grew about 17 percent, producing the modest increase noted in total civilian employment, this growth was largely offset by the declines in other activities. As in many other Western nations, employment in both agriculture and industry declined during this period.

The unemployment rate was 3.9 percent in 1975, 6 percent in 1979, and by the end of December 1980 it had risen to 6.8 percent, a very high level for France. However, the comparisons shown in Table 3 suggest that the French unemployment rates were fairly close to the average for all the EEC countries in 1979 and 1980, and for the third quarter of 1980 the rate appeared to be below those of Italy, Belgium,

*Aspects of the Barre Program*

TABLE 3

Unemployment Rates for Selected European Countries
and the United States, 1975–80

| Country | Unemployment Rate | | |
| | 1975 | 1979 | Third Quarter, 1980 |
| --- | --- | --- | --- |
| West Germany | 4.2% | 3.4% | 3.5% |
| France | 3.9 | 6.0 | 6.4 |
| Italy | 5.3 | 7.5 | 7.9 |
| Netherlands | 4.0 | 4.1 | 4.9 |
| Belgium | 5.3 | 8.7 | 9.5 |
| Luxembourg | 0.2 | 0.7 | 0.7 |
| Great Britain | 3.8 | 5.3 | 7.1 |
| Ireland | 8.5 | 7.9 | 9.2 |
| Denmark | 4.6 | 5.3 | 6.2 |
| United States | 8.5 | 5.8 | 7.6 |
| EEC Average | 4.3 | 5.5 | 6.3 |

*Source:* O. Marchand and J. P. Revoil, "Emploi et chômage: bilan fin 1980," *Economie et statistique* 130 (February 1981):43. Data for 1980 are seasonally adjusted; remaining data are averages for the year of nonseasonally adjusted data.

Great Britain, Ireland, and the United States.[2] Total registered unemployment rose from 933,000 in 1976 to 1,451,000 in 1980, an increase of about 55 percent over the period.

The French unemployment problem is heavily influenced by two factors: the relatively slow real economic growth since 1974 and the large increase in the civilian labor force resulting from the brisk population growth since the end of World War II. Population growth has been encouraged by government policies since the 1930s, when concern about the size of the nation's population began to be widespread. The French population had actually declined in that decade, largely because of the pass-through influence of the 1.3 million Frenchmen killed in World War I. Total population in 1939 was about equal to the 1913 level, and this had been reached only with the aid of massive immigration. The government began a sequence of steps to encourage population growth with the Code de la famille in 1939; by the 1950s and 1960s these included a variety of family allowances which increase with family size, prenatal benefits, maternity grants, government aid with respect to housing, and still other types of assist-

2. Because unemployment is defined differently in various countries and because unemployment data are often compiled from national surveys taken at different times of the year and using different sample designs, unemployment rates across countries can be compared only approximately without extensive adjustments. The data in Table 3 have not been adjusted, while the more detailed data in Table 4 have been adjusted for unemployment definition and can be compared across countries.

ance. These encouragements, together with improving economic conditions and other factors not fully understood, caused the population to grow from an estimated 40 million persons in 1946 (which was less than the population in 1931) to about 53.3 million in 1980, an increase of over 13 million persons, or about 33 percent in 34 years. Moreover, persons born since the end of World War II began to enter the labor force in large numbers at a time when those over 50 years of age were leaving it more slowly. The numbers tell much of the story: about 180,000 new workers joined the labor force each year from 1962 to 1977, resulting in a total of about 2.8 million new workers that had to be absorbed into the labor force over this 16-year period.

A visual impression of the problem posed by the continuing coincidence of strong population growth and relatively weak growth of total employment – the gap between these representing unemployment – can be obtained from Figure 1. Beginning with the year 1955, the active population (as of January 1 each year) and total employment as of the same date are plotted for each year. The distance between a point on the graph of the first of these time series and a point on the second for a given year represents, of course, the number of unemployed persons as of January 1 of the corresponding year. The "unemployment gap" is readily seen to have been widening almost without interruption since 1976. The figure also illustrates the critical role played by the levelling off of employment growth in recent years.[3]

There has also been a rise in labor force participation rates, most notably for women. It has been estimated that between 1968 and 1975 the increase in participation rates for women in the 25-to-54 age group alone caused the labor force to grow by an average of 110,000 per year over this period.[4] Moreover, it is predicted that about 230,000 new job seekers will enter the labor force each year between 1978 and 1985, of which 160,000 are expected to be women.[5]

These comments suggest that the incidence of unemployment should be great among young persons and women; and this is indeed the case in France, as it is in most other EEC nations. Young persons (persons under 25) constitute about 40 percent of the unemployed, and youth unemployment rates tripled from 1970 through 1979 (in contrast to a doubling in the unemployment rate for persons 25 and over). In the fall of 1979 women accounted for about 55 percent of job

3. Figure 1 is taken from M. Boëda, "Les comptes de la Nation de l'année 1980," *Economie et statistique* 135 (July–August 1981), Graphique V, p. 51.

4. Organization for Economic Cooperation and Development, *France* (Paris: OECD, May 1980), p. 56.

5. F. Eymard-Duvernay, "Combien d'actifs d'ici l'an 2000?," *Economie et statistique* 115 (October 1979):36, 42.

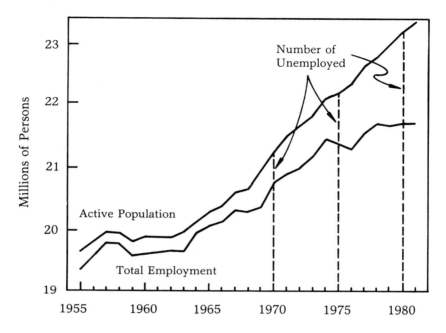

**Figure 1.    Employment, Active Population, and Unemployment,
1955–81**

seekers, although they constituted about 40 percent of the labor force, and about 63 percent of the unemployed youth were women. With respect to another important issue, the duration of unemployment, the average period of unemployment is shorter for young persons but they enter unemployment more frequently than persons 25 and over.[6]

Table 4 displays unemployment rates by age groups in France and selected other countries for 1970–79. Unemployment rates tripled for persons under 25 years of age, reaching 14.2 percent in March 1979; this was true for both teenagers and for persons aged 20 to 24 years. There was some slight improvement in under-25 unemployment from October 1978 to March 1979, particularly for teenagers, but some of this may be due to seasonal influences (see note b at the end of Table 4). The French youth unemployment situation can be contrasted to that in West Germany; although unemployment rates for West

6. François Lagrange, "Unemployment and Manpower Policies in France: Special Schemes for Youth Employment," a paper delivered at the Conference on Critical Economic and Workforce Issues Facing Western Countries, Washington, D.C., December 1979, pp. 2–3.

# TABLE 4

## Unemployment Rate by Age Groups for Selected Countries, 1970–79
### (Numbers are percents)

| Country and Date | All Working Ages | Under Age 25 Total | Under Age 25 Teenagers[a] | Under Age 25 Age 20–24 | Age 25 and Over |
|---|---|---|---|---|---|
| *France*[b] | | | | | |
| March 1970 | 2.5 | 4.8 | 7.0 | 3.7 | 2.0 |
| March 1974 | 2.8 | 6.2 | 9.8 | 4.8 | 2.1 |
| April 1975 | 3.8 | 8.4 | 12.7 | 6.9 | 2.8 |
| March 1976 | 4.5 | 10.8 | 17.0 | 8.6 | 3.3 |
| October 1977 | 5.1 | 13.1 | 21.8 | 9.1 | 3.3 |
| October 1978 | 6.1 | 15.3 | 25.8 | 10.8 | 4.0 |
| March 1979 | 5.7 | 14.2 | 22.7 | 11.4 | 4.1 |
| *West Germany*[c] | | | | | |
| April 1970 | 0.5 | 1.0 | 1.4 | 0.6 | 0.4 |
| April 1974 | 1.2 | 1.8 | 1.9 | 1.7 | 1.1 |
| May 1975 | 2.9 | 4.5 | 4.7 | 4.4 | 2.5 |
| May 1976 | 3.1 | 4.9 | 5.1 | 4.7 | 2.6 |
| April 1977 | 3.2 | 5.0 | 5.0 | 5.0 | 2.7 |
| April 1978 | 3.0 | 4.5 | 4.6 | 4.4 | 2.6 |
| April 1979 | 2.7 | 3.9 | 4.1 | 3.7 | 2.5 |
| *United States* | | | | | |
| 1970 | 4.9 | 11.0 | 15.2 | 8.2 | 3.3 |
| 1974 | 5.6 | 11.8 | 16.0 | 9.0 | 3.6 |
| 1975 | 8.5 | 16.1 | 19.9 | 13.6 | 6.0 |
| 1976 | 7.7 | 14.7 | 19.0 | 12.0 | 5.5 |
| 1977 | 7.0 | 13.6 | 17.7 | 10.9 | 4.9 |
| 1978 | 6.0 | 12.2 | 16.3 | 9.5 | 4.0 |
| 1979 | 5.8 | 11.7 | 16.1 | 9.0 | 3.9 |
| *Italy*[d] | | | | | |
| 1970 | 3.2 | 10.2 | 12.3 | 8.8 | 1.5 |
| 1974 | 2.9 | 11.2 | 14.3 | 9.1 | 1.2 |
| 1975 | 3.4 | 12.9 | 16.8 | 10.4 | 1.5 |
| 1976 | 3.7 | 14.6 | 19.2 | 11.7 | 1.6 |
| 1977 | 4.6 | 17.7 | 22.9 | 14.3 | 1.9 |
| 1978 | 5.0 | 19.4 | 25.2 | 15.8 | 2.0 |
| *Canada* | | | | | |
| 1970 | 5.7 | 10.0 | 13.9 | 7.5 | 4.2 |
| 1974 | 5.3 | 9.3 | 11.6 | 7.6 | 3.9 |
| 1975 | 6.9 | 12.0 | 14.9 | 9.9 | 5.0 |
| 1976 | 7.1 | 12.7 | 15.7 | 10.5 | 5.1 |
| 1977 | 8.1 | 14.4 | 17.5 | 12.2 | 5.8 |
| 1978 | 8.4 | 14.5 | 17.9 | 12.2 | 6.1 |
| 1979 | 7.5 | 13.0 | 16.1 | 10.8 | 5.4 |

TABLE 4 *(continued)*

| Country and Date | All Working Ages | Under Age 25 | | | Age 25 and Over |
|---|---|---|---|---|---|
| | | Total | Teenagers[a] | Age 20–24 | |
| *United Kingdom*[e] | | | | | |
| July 1971 | 3.0 | 4.5 | 5.3 | 4.0 | 2.6 |
| July 1974 | 2.3 | 3.8 | 4.5 | 3.3 | 2.0 |
| July 1975 | 4.1 | 9.2 | 12.0 | 7.3 | 2.9 |
| July 1976 | 5.5 | 13.0 | 20.1 | 8.0 | 3.8 |
| July 1977 | 6.0 | 14.7 | 23.2 | 8.9 | 4.0 |
| July 1978 | 5.8 | 13.9 | 22.1 | 8.2 | 4.0 |
| July 1979 | 5.3 | 12.3 | 19.1 | 7.6 | 3.7 |

*Source:* C. Sorrentino, "Youth Unemployment: An International Perspective," *Monthly Labor Review* 104 (July 1981), Table 1, p. 5.

*Notes:* Unemployment rates have been adjusted in an attempt to make data comparable to U.S. concepts and definitions of unemployment and thus comparable across countries; data are annual averages except where otherwise indicated.

[a] Teenagers include 16- to 19-year-olds in the U.S., France, and United Kingdom (1974 onwards); 15- to 19-year-olds in Canada, West Germany, and United Kingdom (prior to 1974); 14- to 19-year-olds in Italy.

[b] French unemployment rates for March or April are usually lower than annual averages and October rates are usually above annual averages.

[c] April or May rates for West Germany are somewhat less than annual averages.

[d] Data adjustment problems exist for Italy; see Sorrentino, p. 5.

[e] United Kingdom data are for the registered unemployed.

German youths were also considerably higher in 1979 than in 1970, unemployment rates in West Germany for all age groups showed improvement from 1977 to 1979.

Another way to assess youth unemployment is in terms of the age distribution of the unemployed and of the labor force. In March 1979, 39 percent of French unemployment was attributable to persons under 25 years of age, yet these persons constituted 16 percent of the labor force (see corresponding portions of Table 5). Alternatively, persons in the 20-to-24 age group constituted 24 percent of the unemployed and yet were only 12 percent of the labor force.

What steps did the government take in the face of these enormous problems? It avoided demand stimulation-style macroeconomic policies, apparently because it believed that they would have unfavorable impacts on the price level and on the balance of payments, which in turn would have the effect of worsening the unemployment situation beyond the short term. Instead, it developed measures aimed at specific employment problems, particularly the generation of employment for young persons, women, and persons over 45 years of age

TABLE 5

Percent Distribution of Unemployment and
Labor Force, France, 1963–79

|  | March 1963 | March 1970 | March 1974 | April 1975 | March 1976 | March 1977 | March 1978 | March 1979 |
|---|---|---|---|---|---|---|---|---|
| *Unemployment* | | | | | | | | |
| Under Age 25 | 35 | 37 | 39 | 39 | 40 | 41 | 39 | 39 |
| Teenagers | 22 | 17 | 17 | 16 | 16 | 16 | 15 | 15 |
| Age 20–24 | 13 | 20 | 22 | 23 | 24 | 25 | 24 | 24 |
| Age 25 and over | 65 | 63 | 61 | 61 | 60 | 59 | 61 | 61 |
| *Labor Force* | | | | | | | | |
| Under Age 25 | 18 | 19 | 18 | 18 | 17 | 17 | 16 | 16 |
| Teenagers | 8 | 6 | 5 | 5 | 4 | 4 | 4 | 4 |
| Age 20–24 | 10 | 13 | 13 | 13 | 13 | 13 | 12 | 12 |
| Age 25 and over | 82 | 81 | 82 | 82 | 83 | 83 | 84 | 84 |

Source: Sorrentino, Table 2, p. 7. Percents rounded so as to add to 100.

who had been unemployed for more than one year. These measures were set forth in the "national employment pact" (*pacte national pour l'emploi des jeunes*) in 1977. This was followed by a second pact in July 1978 and by a third in July 1979. The principal feature of these arrangements is that employers are granted a partial and temporary exemption from the social security contributions they are required to pay for their employees (such contributions are a considerable business expense). Under the second pact, for example, businesses employing fewer than 500 persons or having a turnover of less than 100 million francs were exempted for a 12-month period from half of the usual employers' contributions for each person between 21 and 26 employed between July 1978 and December 1979 and for each female employee who was widowed, divorced in the preceding two years, or unmarried and who had at least one dependent child. During the same 17-month period, recruitment of apprentices carried a complete exemption from employers' contributions for a period of 12 months, and subsidies were also made available to employers for the recruitment of persons over 45 who had been unemployed for more than a year and for persons newly employed in craft enterprises. Encouragement of on-the-job training and incentives for offering practical courses of instruction, originally developed for selected enterprises and industrial sectors in the 1977 pact, were extended to all industries and sectors in the second pact.

The pacts were funded out of budget appropriations, and substantial sums were involved: 3.5 billion francs for the first pact, 1.3 billion for the second, and 3.2 billion for the third. According to government estimates, the first pact "benefitted" 553,000 persons, the second 275,000, and the third about 250,000. There have as yet been no studies which provide reliable assessments of how much employment of other than a purely temporary kind has actually been created by these measures. As we have seen, both the total number of unemployed and the unemployment rate continued to rise significantly throughout the period in which these pacts were in operation. There is some evidence that business firms have used pact-related employment to fill jobs for given, often short, periods of time, to enhance their flexibility to adjust labor force needs without altering the number of permanent workers (the latter would arouse the opposition of labor unions). In 1979 more than one-third of the young persons who registered with the National Employment Agency had done so at the end of an interim job or upon the termination of a contract to work for a fixed period of time.[7]

Up to now we have been concerned with what might be called a standard rendition of influences contributing to unemployment. Three other factors also contribute to unemployment, or to what is largely the same thing in the current French context, the slow rise in total employment: the collection of rigid redundancy or lay-off regulations (usually designed to enhance job security for the currently employed), the sequence of sharp rises in the minimum wage or SMIC (which can spill over into other wage rates and influence the quantity of labor services demanded by firms, as well as other aspects of the labor market), and the considerable size of the payments made by firms (in the form of direct employment-associated taxes) into government unemployment compensation programs and general social security benefit fund sources. Unfortunately, it is extremely difficult to estimate or to quantify even crudely the effects of each of these factors and to assign portions of unemployment growth to them (or to quantify how these factors have contributed to the moderation of total employment growth), although much research is being done in both Western Europe and the United States on one of these topics, the economics of legal minimum wages. Although there is considerable agreement that all three of these factors have risen in importance since 1973, opinions on the relative contribution of each naturally vary. Moreover, careful studies and sound research findings concerning the role of these factors in the French economy are hard to come by. We will make brief comments on the first of these factors, omitting the second and third because they would take us further into a

---

7. Ibid., p. 3; see also Organization for Economic Cooperation and Development, *France* (Paris: OECD, February 1979), pp. 43–48.

consideration of labor economics, labor market structures, social security policies, and political features of French life than is appropriate for a study of this kind.[8]

With respect to layoff regulations, if a French firm wishes to discharge workers it must make an application to do so, and this must pass through the workers' union (if one is involved) and then be referred to a labor inspector (*inspecteur du travail*) employed by the government. This request must be supported by information concerning the financial status of the firm, why each worker is being considered for termination, etc. The inspectors are often regarded by managers as pro-labor; it seems reasonable that, whatever the issues may be in a particular case that is brought before them, they would have some interest, either personal or vested, in helping to reduce unemployment, perhaps in the context of a local or regional employment problem. In any event, the administrative process can consume up to six months or more, and such delays and associated uncertainties and expenses can escalate management problems relating to organizational efficiency and productivity by increasing the difficulty of laying off workers—which, in turn, will exert downward influences on new hire decisions as well. They may also increase the substitution of part-time and temporary employment for full-time employment and thus contribute to some of the problems noted earlier in this section.[9]

A related aspect of the layoff problem and its effect on new job creation has been summarized by an American student of the situation in the following way:

8. A Fourçans, in "L'Impact du SMIC sur le chômage: les leçons de l'éxperience," *Revue d'économie politique* 6 (1980):881–93, employed a regression model to estimate the percent of the increase in youth unemployment of males and females accounted for by the rise in the purchasing power of SMIC. He concluded that the rapid increase in SMIC over the period 1973–77 probably raised unemployment and that the incidence of this increase was greatest among males and females under 25 years of age (and between young males and females, greater among males). R. Rosa ("The Effects of Minimum Wage Regulation in France," in *The Economics of Legal Minimum Wages,* ed. S. Rottenberg [Washington, D.C.: American Enterprise Institute for Public Policy Research, 1981], pp. 357–76) develops a collection of regression models to assess the impact of SMIC (see pp. 369–74); but since the Durbin-Watson statistic for each model is either indeterminate or indicates positive (first-order) autocorrelation, his empirical results appear to be unreliable. For further comments on current research and various points of view in minimum wage economics, see the notes following this chapter.

9. Rigid lay-off regulations are by no means limited to France. Since the recession of 1974, management prerogatives to dismiss workers have been substantially curtailed in West Germany and the United Kingdom as well as in France. Moreover, lay-off regulations may exacerbate youth unemployment problems; a study done in West Germany indicated that regulations designed to protect senior workers have raised youth unemployment, and similar views have been expressed in Sweden and Italy. See C. Sorrentino, "Youth Unemployment: An International Perspective," *Monthly Labor Review* 104 (July 1981):10–11.

The unions may well be as important as the bureaucracy in influencing the entrepreneur's calculations about the cost of lay-offs. For example, an industrialist with one plant in a communist-run suburb of Paris and another in Normandy who wished to close the former and concentrate operations in the latter expected to receive authorization [from the *inspecteurs*] to do so, since the town was lost to the majority [political party] in any event. But he realized that the unions would occupy the plant he shut, and the troubles might well spread to the plant in Normandy. So despite the financial precariousness of his firm he kept both plants open. An official of one of France's largest companies argued that the basic constraint on their personnel reductions was not the state but the C.G.T. [Confédération générale du travail], with whom management has a complex, unwritten set of understandings: "We only do what the unions, at the limit, will accept."[10]

A discussion of unemployment should not omit a related issue of considerable importance, the problem of how unemployment is measured. Unemployment statistics in most Western nations attempt to measure the number of persons who are not working but who are actively seeking work. Thus, persons who are unemployed, who are available for and desire employment but who, for a variety of reasons, think they cannot find it and do not actively search for jobs, are not counted among the unemployed. The number of such persons, who are called discouraged workers or the "silent reserve," is not known with accuracy, but studies in various countries suggest that it is far from trivial. A study estimated that there were nearly one million discouraged workers in the U.S. during the first quarter of 1978; moreover, labor force studies in France and Sweden as well as in the U.S. have indicated that teenagers and young adults (persons from 20 to 24 years of age) constitute a large portion of the pool of discouraged workers in these countries.[11] Another measurement problem is that unemployment statistics in such countries as France and West Germany do not take into consideration the number of foreign workers who become unemployed and subsequently emigrate. Studies have also shown that a large portion of such emigrants are under 25 years of age.

These influences may serve to make the unemployment statistic (or "recorded unemployment") a smaller number than it might be if additional information were available on discouraged workers. On the other hand, there are other influences which can contribute to the

10. S. Berger, "Lame Ducks and National Champions: Industrial Policy in the Fifth Republic," in *The Fifth Republic at Twenty*, ed. W. G. Andrews and S. Hoffmann (Albany: State University of New York Press, 1981), p. 304.
11. See Sorrentino, p. 9; T. A. Finegan, "Improving Our Information on Discouraged Workers," *Monthly Labor Review*, September 1978, pp. 15–25; Organization for Economic Cooperation and Development, *Youth Unemployment: Causes and Consequences* (Paris: OECD, 1980); M. S. Gordon, *Youth Education and Unemployment Problems* (Berkeley, Cal.: Carnegie Council on Policy Studies in Higher Education, 1979).

increase in recorded unemployment: the existence of other forms of nonwage income, including the income of a spouse, and unemployment compensation payments to workers. Recent studies in the U.S. have shown that one effect of unemployment compensation is to lengthen the period of search for a job and thereby increase recorded unemployment. The existence of a spouse's income can have similar effects, or it can be an important reason why an unemployed person is not seeking a job. Newer theories of wage bargaining have attempted to incorporate such influences.[12]

## Inflation, Wages, Profits, and Real Economic Growth

Other aspects of the Barre program also turned out to be less successful than had been hoped. Efforts to reduce inflation were largely frustrated; one indication is that the CPI increased by more than 9 percent in 1977 and 1978, rose above 10 percent in 1979, and exceeded 13 percent in 1980. France's inflation performance since 1975 has been roughly similar to that of some other Western nations, and her CPI annual percentage increases have been close to the average of the 20 nations forming the OECD area. France's CPI increases were below the average of the EEC countries from 1975 through 1977 but were above the latter by one percentage point or more for 1978, 1979, and 1980 (see Table 6).

Inflation problems escalated, it should be stressed, despite the fact that effective demand was growing more slowly than in the 15-year period prior to 1976 and despite the existence of considerable spare

TABLE 6

Year-to-Year Percent Increases in CPI, 1975-79

| Country/Region | 1975 | 1976 | 1977 | 1978 | 1979 | 1980 |
|---|---|---|---|---|---|---|
| France | 11.8 | 9.6 | 9.5 | 9.3 | 10.7 | 13.6 |
| OECD Area Weighted Average | 11.2 | 8.6 | 9.1 | 8.3 | 10.9 | 12.8 |
| EEC Area Weighted Average | 12.6 | 10.3 | 10.2 | 7.3 | 9.6 | 12.4 |

*Source:* Organization for Economic Cooperation and Development, *Main Economic Indicators* (Paris: OECD, October 1981), pp. 104, 165.

*Note:* For the OECD and EEC areas, prices are weighted by final private consumption in each constituent country. The EEC countries are Belgium, Denmark, France, West Germany, Ireland, Italy, Luxembourg, Netherlands, and United Kingdom (Greece became a member on January 1, 1981). The OECD area consists of more than 20 European and selected non-European countries; the list of country names is given in OECD, *France,* May 1980, p. 79.

12. On these and other related issues, see R. M. Solow, "On Theories of Unemployment," *American Economic Review* 70 (March 1980):1–11.

capacity in the economy. The latter, however, must be interpreted with great care, because the problem of defining capacity, never simple, has been compounded – perhaps beyond comprehension – by the sharp increases in energy prices experienced since 1974. Much productive capacity in France and other countries has been outmoded and can no longer be utilized at current energy price levels. It is estimated, for example, that the oil price increase of 1974 lowered U.S. capacity by about 4.5 percent by the end of 1976. Moreover, average rates of return on past investment may also have fallen, making it even more difficult for many firms to finance new investments, even when the marginal productivity of new investment is high. It may also be the case that the required rate of return on new investment has risen because of increasing uncertainty generated by the prospect of continuing high inflation rates and their impact on future cost-price relationships. Furthermore, owing to the condition of the French capital stock in 1974, it could be the case that the obsolescence caused by the rise in energy prices has had a much more severe effect on French productivity than is currently suspected, but research on this question or on the others mentioned above has not come to the writer's attention.

The government also made only limited progress in dealing with the extraordinarily difficult problem of restraining wage and salary increases to the rise in the CPI (or to the levels which were consistent with the underlying rate of growth in productivity and continuing balance of payments constraints). Hourly wage growth has been rapid since the early 1970s and is an element in inflation, as are the wage indexation system in France and her strong import demand. The latter, it is often asserted, contributes to the importing of inflation from other countries.

Wage rate growth can be examined from several different points of view. Table 7 shows year-to-year percent changes in the CPI and in an index of hourly wage rates in manufacturing. Increases in the wage rate uniformly exceed the former, although the gap between these has been less in recent years than in 1975 and 1976.

Table 8 indicates that the index of all hourly wage rates also exceeded the annual percent changes in the CPI from 1974–79, as did those for the minimum wage. Of the categories shown, only salaries in public services were below the increase in CPI and only for one of the years shown, 1979.

Yet another view of the movement in real wages is provided by a consideration of real compensation (which includes wages plus fringe benefits) per employed worker since the early 1970s. This is plotted in Figure 2, which also shows real national income per employed

TABLE 7

Year-to-Year Percent Changes in CPI and Hourly Wage
Rates in Manufacturing, France, 1974–80

| Year | CPI | Percent Change in CPI | Hourly Wage Rates in Manufacturing | Percent Change in Hourly Rates |
|---|---|---|---|---|
| 1974 | 89.50 | 13.72 | 85.30 | 19.30 |
| 1975 | 100.00 | 11.73 | 100.00 | 17.23 |
| 1976 | 109.60 | 9.60 | 114.10 | 14.10 |
| 1977 | 119.90 | 9.34 | 128.50 | 12.62 |
| 1978 | 130.80 | 9.09 | 145.20 | 13.00 |
| 1979 | 144.80 | 10.70 | 164.10 | 13.02 |
| 1980 | 164.50 | 13.60 | 188.80 | 15.05 |

*Sources:* Organization for Economic Cooperation and Development, *Main Economic Indicators,* 1960–79 (Paris: OECD, 1980), pp. 294, 296; *Main Economic Indicators,* October 1981, p. 104.

TABLE 8

Wage Rate Developments, 1974–79

| | Average Percent Change 1974–76 | Percent Change from Previous Year | | |
| | | 1977 | 1978 | 1979 |
|---|---|---|---|---|
| Consumers Price Index | 10.7[a] | 9.3 | 9.1 | 10.7 |
| Index of Hourly Wage Rates | 17.1 | 12.7 | 12.6 | 13.0 |
| Index of Hourly Wage Rates in Manufacturing | 17.1 | 12.8 | 13.0 | 13.0 |
| Minimum Hourly Wage (SMIC) | 19.0 | 12.7 | 12.9 | 12.5 |
| General Index of Salaries in the Public Service | 14.9 | 10.0 | 10.6 | 9.6 |
| Changes in Purchasing Power | | | | |
| Hourly Wage Rate | 4.8 | 2.9 | 3.1 | 2.1 |
| Minimum Wage | 6.5 | 2.9 | 3.3 | 1.7 |
| Salaries in Public Service | 2.8 | 0.5 | 1.2 | −0.9 |

*Sources:* Calculations from data in Table 7; OECD, *France,* May 1980, Table 4, p. 22.
[a] Compound annual growth rate for period.

worker.[13] A comparison of these two time series sheds light on the contrast between the growth of compensation and the growth of incomes. Prior to 1973 these two variables grew at similar rates; by late 1973, however, a gap began to appear between them as the former continued to grow at steep rates while the latter declined. Moreover, when the latter resumed an upward path its slope was initially less

13. Figure 2 is taken from OECD, *France,* May 1980, diagram 6, p. 23.

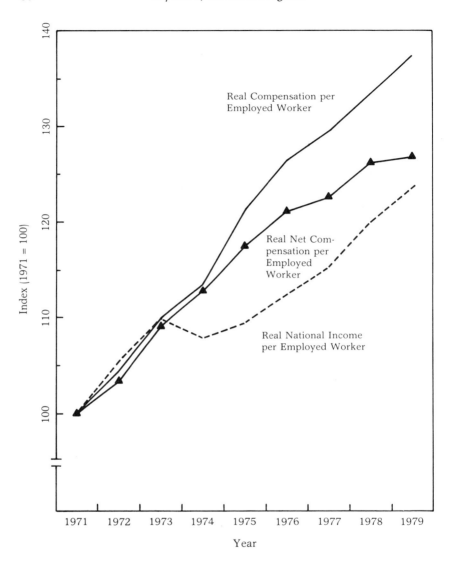

**Figure 2.    Real Compensation, Real Net Compensation, and
Real National Income per Employed Worker, 1971–79**

steep than that for compensation; and although the rates of growth in
the two variables have been comparable in recent years, the gap has
not narrowed since 1975. A major portion of this gap, however, can
be attributed to the growth of social security contributions, which are
part of the total compensation of workers. If the social security contributions of employers and employees are deleted, the result is net

compensation. Figure 2 also shows real net compensation per employed worker, and it is readily apparent that the gap between this time series and real national income per employed worker has been narrowing since 1976.

The struggle against inflation and the strenuous efforts to stabilize the franc have been important influences in the modest increase in real economic growth compared to pre-1973 levels. Table 9 indicates that annual real GDP growth in the period 1959–73 was often above 5 percent and sometimes topped 6 percent; in contrast, it averaged 3.41 percent per year during 1977–1979 (year over year) and was 1.64 percent in 1980. This table also indicates that the growth rate for 1973–80 was about half that in the periods 1959–66 and 1966–73.

The slackening of real GDP growth rates for the post-1973 period as

TABLE 9

Real Gross Domestic Product, 1970 Prices
(In billions of francs)

| Year | Real GDP | Percent Change from Previous Year |
|---|---|---|
| 1959 | 424.8 | . . . . |
| 1960 | 455.2 | 7.16 |
| 1961 | 480.3 | 5.51 |
| 1962 | 512.4 | 6.68 |
| 1963 | 539.7 | 5.33 |
| 1964 | 574.9 | 6.52 |
| 1965 | 602.4 | 4.78 |
| 1966 | 633.8 | 5.21 |
| 1967 | 663.5 | 4.69 |
| 1968 | 691.8 | 4.27 |
| 1969 | 740.1 | 6.98 |
| 1970 | 782.5 | 5.73 |
| 1971 | 824.9 | 5.42 |
| 1972 | 873.5 | 5.89 |
| 1973 | 920.4 | 5.37 |
| 1974 | 950.2 | 3.24 |
| 1975 | 952.0 | 0.19 |
| 1976 | 1001.2 | 5.17 |
| 1977 | 1031.7 | 3.05 |
| 1978 | 1070.0 | 3.71 |
| 1979 | 1107.0 | 3.46 |
| 1980 | 1125.1 | 1.64 |

*Compound Annual Growth Rates*
| | | |
|---|---|---|
| 1959–66 | 5.88 | |
| 1966–73 | 5.47 | |
| 1973–80 | 2.91 | |

Sources: For 1959–75, Les Collections de l'INSEE, *Rapport sur les comptes de la nation de l'année 1979* (Paris: INSEE, 1980), Tome C, "Comptes et planification," pp. 214–15. For 1976–80, OECD, *Quarterly National Accounts Bulletin, 1981/II* (Paris: OECD, 1981), p. 54.

contrasted to the pre-1973 period is not unique to France. The phenomenon is shared to a great extent by other Western nations, by countries in eastern Europe, by the U.S.S.R., and to some extent even by Japan. For example, the growth rates for France for the 1977–80 period were about the same as a weighted average of France's major trading partners; they were above those for the EEC in this period; and in 1980, a bad year for France, real growth exceeded that in the United States, the U.K., and Canada, and equalled real growth in West Germany. These and other data are shown in Table 10. It is interesting to note that the real growth rate in Japan for 1980, 5.0 percent, although the largest shown for this year, is considerably less than for the same country in 1973 and is less than half the average (11.3 percent) for the period 1961–72. Table 11 gives another performance measure, per-capita real GNP growth rates, and similar declining patterns during the 1975–80 period can be observed for several Western countries, notably the United States, Italy, and the Netherlands.

These data suggest that the latter half of the 1970s was a painful period for most Western nations and that the French economy per-

TABLE 10

Growth Rates in Real Gross National Product, 1961–80
(Percent change from preceding year)

| Country/ Region | Annual Average 1961–72 | 1973 | 1974 | 1975 | 1976 | 1977 | 1978 | 1979 | 1980 |
|---|---|---|---|---|---|---|---|---|---|
| France | 6.2 | 5.3 | 3.2 | 0.2 | 5.2 | 2.8 | 3.6 | 3.3 | 1.8 |
| West Germany | 5.1 | 5.1 | 0.4 | − 1.8 | 5.3 | 2.6 | 3.5 | 4.5 | 1.8 |
| Italy | 5.5 | 6.8 | 4.1 | − 3.6 | 5.9 | 1.9 | 2.6 | 5.0 | 3.8 |
| United Kingdom | 3.0 | 6.0 | − 1.2 | − 0.8 | 4.2 | 1.0 | 3.6 | 1.5 | − 2.3 |
| United States | 4.3 | 5.4 | − 0.6 | − 1.1 | 5.4 | 5.5 | 4.8 | 3.2 | − 0.2 |
| Japan | 11.3 | 9.8 | − 0.6 | 1.5 | 6.5 | 5.4 | 6.0 | 5.9 | 5.0 |
| Canada | 5.9 | 7.2 | 3.6 | 1.2 | 5.5 | 2.2 | 3.4 | 2.8 | − 0.5 |
| EEC | 4.9 | 5.2 | 1.7 | − 1.3 | 5.2 | 2.3 | 3.2 | 3.5 | 1.0 |

Sources: Data for 1961–72 and 1973 from Economic Report of the President, January 1978, Table B-107, p. 380; data for 1974–80 from Economic Report of the President, January 1981, Table B-107, p. 353 (data for 1980 are preliminary estimates).

Notes: Data for France, Italy, and the United Kingdom are for Gross Domestic Product. "Real" means adjusted for inflation. Various countries use deflators having different years as bases – for example, France, West Germany, and Italy use 1970; Japan and the United Kingdom use 1975; the United States uses 1972; and Canada uses 1971.

formed relatively well compared to those of the other nations shown. Even the "wonder economy" of West Germany, so long the productivity and output leader of western Europe, was experiencing heavy weather by 1980, incurring balance of payments deficits for the first time in about 30 years (in January 1981 West Germany had its largest monthly trade deficit since World War II).

The situation with respect to investment and business profits is difficult to assess. Although gross fixed capital formation in 1979 amounted to about 21 percent of GDP, giving France one of the highest proportions in the Western world, increasingly substantial amounts of investment were going to public enterprises and households during the 1970s and private industry's share declined. Table 12 shows percent shares for 1970 and 1979 and indicates that large public enterprises, services and commercial activities, and households

TABLE 11

Per-Capita Real GNP Growth Rates, 1970–80
(Percent change from preceding year)

| Year | France | United States | West Germany | Italy | Netherlands | United Kingdom | Japan | Canada |
|---|---|---|---|---|---|---|---|---|
| 1970 | 4.8 | -1.2 | 4.9 | 4.6 | 5.1 | 2.0 | 10.6 | 1.1 |
| 1975 | -0.3 | 9.1 | -1.4 | -4.3 | -2.7 | -0.7 | 0.2 | -0.3 |
| 1976 | 4.8 | 4.6 | 5.8 | 5.2 | 4.7 | 3.9 | 4.1 | 4.2 |
| 1977 | 2.7 | 4.6 | 3.1 | 1.4 | 1.8 | 1.0 | 4.3 | 1.0 |
| 1978 | 3.3 | 3.9 | 3.7 | 2.2 | 1.5 | 3.6 | 4.1 | 2.8 |
| 1979 | 3.1 | 2.3 | 4.5 | 4.5 | 1.6 | 1.0 | 4.7 | 2.2 |
| 1980 | 1.2 | -1.0 | 1.5 | 3.7 | 0.4 | * | 3.4 | -1.0 |

*Source:* U.S. Department of Commerce, *International Economic Indicators* (Washington, D.C.: Government Printing Office, September 1981), p. 7.
*Notes:* GDP rather than GNP is used for France, Italy, and the United Kingdom.
* Not available.

TABLE 12

Selected Percent Shares of
Gross Fixed Capital Formation, 1970 and 1979

| Type of Activity | 1970 | 1979 |
|---|---|---|
| Large Public Enterprises | 8.3 | 12.2 |
| Services and Commercial Activities | 10.5 | 11.0 |
| Households | 23.2 | 27.1 |
| Private Industry | 20.2 | 14.9 |

*Source:* C. Gross, "L'Investissement industriel en France, son evolution, son financement," *Etudes de Banque de France,* 1979, p. 10.

each increased their shares over this period, while that of private industry decreased substantially (from 20.2 percent to 14.9 percent). Investment in private industry has been stagnating in other ways since 1973. The level of private investment declined in 1974 and 1975; and although investment performance since 1976 has improved relative to the levels in these years, the 1980 level was about what it had been in 1970 and was about 10 percent less than the level reached in 1973.[14]

Another view of investment performance can be obtained by considering the relationship between gross fixed capital formation and value added in various economic sectors. Table 13 displays such ratios (expressed as a percent of value added) in terms of 1970 prices. The data for all business sectors indicate that the ratio rose in 1969–73 as compared with 1963–68, but declined again in the period 1974–80 to a level slightly below that attained in 1963–68. When large national enterprises are excluded from the calculations (see second row of Table 13), the decline for 1974–80 was even larger (1.6 percentage points as against 0.9 percentage point), suggesting that the decline in the average investment rate for private business firms was nearly twice that for national enterprises.

The unfavorable situation for industry noted elsewhere in this monograph is also confirmed by the data in this table. The decline from 1969–73 to 1974–80 was greatest for industry (2.9 percentage points), as was the decline from the earliest to the latest period (2.3 percentage points).

The profits situation remains mixed despite the removal of price controls and the effects of other policies that were designed under the Barre program to help businesses. It is difficult to summarize this situation because profit data on French firms are sparse. One view of profit performance in the French economy is provided by Table 14, which expresses major balance sheet expense items in terms of value added for private nonagricultural firms. The gross margin rate (ratio of gross margin to value added) provides a crude measure of profits relative to value added for such firms. The table also shows an allocation of the gross margin rate to other expense items and indicates the gross margin retained in these firms (all in terms of value added). The considerable increase in employers' social security contributions is evident, as are the disturbing declines since 1973 in the gross margin rate (4.6 percentage points) and in the gross margin retained (2.3 percentage points).

14. C. Gross, "L'Investissement industriel en France, son evolution, son financement," *Etudes de Banque de France*, 1979, p. 11.

TABLE 13

Average Rate of Productive Investment by Economic Sector
for Selected Periods in 1970 Prices

| Economic Sector | 1963–68 | 1969–73 | 1974–80 | 1974–80 Percent Minus 1969–73 Percent (Percentage Points) | 1974–80 Percent Minus 1963–68 Percent (Percentage Points) |
|---|---|---|---|---|---|
| All Business Sectors | 12.2% | 13.0% | 12.1% | –0.9 | –0.1 |
| All Business Sectors except Large National Enterprises | 9.7 | 11.0 | 9.4 | –1.6 | –0.3 |
| Industry | 16.4 | 17.0 | 14.1 | –2.9 | –2.3 |
| Commercial Services | 8.3 | 11.3 | 10.5 | –0.8 | +2.2 |

*Source:* M. Boëda, "Les Comptes de la Nation de l'année 1980," *Economie et statistique* 135 (July–August 1981):48.

*Note:* Average rate of productive investment is gross fixed capital divided by value added.

## TABLE 14

### Distribution of Value Added in Private, Nonagricultural Firms, 1973–80

| Category | 1973 | 1974 | 1975 | 1976 | 1977 | 1978 | 1979 | 1980 |
|---|---|---|---|---|---|---|---|---|
| Gross Salaries | 49.8% | 50.9% | 51.7% | 52.0% | 51.5% | 51.4% | 50.4% | 51.4% |
| Employers' Social Security Contributions | 14.6 | 15.1 | 16.8 | 17.1 | 17.3 | 17.5 | 17.9 | 18.3 |
| Indirect Taxes less Subsidies | 8.0 | 6.9 | 6.8 | 6.4 | 6.8 | 6.9 | 7.4 | 7.3 |
| Gross Margin Rate (Ratio of Gross Margin to Value Added) | 27.6 | 27.1 | 24.7 | 24.5 | 24.4 | 24.2 | 24.3 | 23.0 |
| Totals | 100.0% | 100.0% | 100.0% | 100.0% | 100.0% | 100.0% | 100.0% | 100.0% |
| Major Components of Gross Margin Rate | | | | | | | | |
| Taxes on Profits | 3.7 | 4.6 | 3.1 | 3.7 | 4.1 | 3.4 | 3.6 | 4.1 |
| Dividends and Miscellaneous | 5.9 | 5.5 | 5.4 | 4.8 | 4.5 | 4.5 | 4.1 | 3.8 |
| Net Interest Paid | 5.6 | 6.9 | 6.2 | 5.7 | 5.6 | 5.2 | 5.0 | 5.0 |
| Gross Margin Retained in Businesses | 12.4 | 10.1 | 10.0 | 10.3 | 10.2 | 11.1 | 11.6 | 10.1 |
| Totals | 27.6% | 27.1% | 24.7% | 24.5% | 24.4% | 24.2% | 24.3% | 23.0% |

*Source:* Boëda, p. 53.

*Note:* Gross margin rate = *excédent brut d'exploitation ou taux de marge*; gross margin retained = *épargne brute ou taux d'épargne* (for firms).

# Productivity Developments and Problems

Recently published research studies of productivity in France and other developed nations indicate that productivity growth has followed patterns similar to those of real economic growth noted in the preceding section: rates of increase for periods within the interval 1959–73 were consistently higher than those for periods since 1973 (although there was already some deceleration by the late 1960s for the United States and Italy). All of these findings relate to private (business) sectors, and more particularly in several cases to manufacturing, because data for other economic sectors, notably government and services, are inadequate, misleading, or nonexistent. Fortunately, the private sector accounts for most of the GDP or GNP generation in the countries considered, so that after 1973 rates of change in GDP from all sources and from the private sector are very similar except for Sweden and the United Kingdom, where private sector growth was significantly less than for GDP.[15]

Table 15 shows average annual percent changes in real gross business product (i.e., private sector portions of GDP or GNP) and in private factor input quantities and factor productivities. The real product estimates in this table are mostly in terms of 1975 prices, although for some countries relative price weights for earlier years are used.[16] The time interval 1960–79 is subdivided into the subperiods 1960–73 and 1973–79 because of the separating property of the landmark year, 1973.

Percent changes in both real gross business product and total factor productivities declined for each country in the later period. However, when countries are ranked in terms of percent changes in total factor productivities for each period, as in Table 16, one sees that France ranks fourth out of nine for the earlier period and is tied for second, with West Germany, in the later one. Surprisingly, France turns out to do very well according to these measures, and is well above the average performance of the countries examined for both periods. More surprisingly still, according to the factor productivities measure for 1973–79, France outranks Japan.

Turning to a consideration of the manufacturing sector, productivity (in terms of output per hour) slowed in the 1973–80 period in con-

15. J. Kendrick, "International Comparisons of Recent Productivity Trends," in *Essays in Contemporary Economic Problems, Demand, Productivity, and Population*, 1981–82 edition, ed. W. Fellner (Washington, D.C.: American Enterprise Institute for Public Policy Research, 1981), p. 127.

16. Data are from OECD sources; see Kendrick, pp. 127–33, for a discussion of the data and of the Denison-type growth accounting model used in developing the requisite estimates.

TABLE 15

Real Gross Business Product, Business Factor Inputs,
and Productivities of Selected Countries, 1960–79
(Average annual percentage change)

| Country | Real Gross Business Product | Factor Inputs | | | Factor Productivities | | |
|---|---|---|---|---|---|---|---|
| | | Total | Labor | Capital | Total | Labor | Capital |
| France | | | | | | | |
| 1960–73 | 5.8 | 1.9 | −0.1 | 5.1 | 3.9 | 5.9 | 0.7 |
| 1973–79 | 3.2 | 1.1 | −1.0 | 4.3 | 2.1 | 4.2 | −1.1 |
| West Germany | | | | | | | |
| 1960–73 | 4.6 | 1.4 | −1.2 | 6.1 | 3.2 | 5.8 | −1.5 |
| 1973–79 | 2.2 | 0.1 | −2.1 | 4.1 | 2.1 | 4.3 | −1.9 |
| Japan | | | | | | | |
| 1960–73 | 10.8 | 4.2 | 0.9 | 10.9 | 6.6 | 9.9 | 0.1 |
| 1973–79 | 4.2 | 2.4 | 0.4 | 6.4 | 1.8 | 3.8 | −2.2 |
| Belgium | | | | | | | |
| 1960–73 | 5.3 | 1.1 | −0.8 | 4.4 | 4.2 | 6.1 | 0.9 |
| 1973–79 | 2.1 | −0.5 | −2.3 | 2.7 | 2.6 | 4.4 | −0.6 |
| Italy | | | | | | | |
| 1960–73 | 5.6 | −0.2 | −2.2 | 4.3 | 5.8 | 7.8 | 1.3 |
| 1973–79 | 2.6 | 1.8 | 1.0 | 3.4 | 0.8 | 1.6 | −0.8 |
| Sweden | | | | | | | |
| 1960–73 | 4.2 | 0.6 | −1.6 | 4.1 | 3.6 | 5.8 | 0.1 |
| 1973–79 | 0.1 | −0.2 | −2.4 | 3.4 | 0.3 | 2.5 | −3.3 |
| United States | | | | | | | |
| 1960–73 | 4.4 | 2.5 | 1.3 | 4.5 | 1.9 | 3.1 | −0.1 |
| 1973–79 | 2.9 | 2.3 | 1.8 | 3.1 | 0.6 | 1.1 | −0.2 |
| Canada | | | | | | | |
| 1960–73 | 5.8 | 2.9 | 1.6 | 4.7 | 2.9 | 4.2 | 1.1 |
| 1973–79 | 3.2 | 3.3 | 2.2 | 4.8 | −0.1 | 1.0 | −1.6 |
| United Kingdom | | | | | | | |
| 1960–73 | 2.9 | 0.7 | −0.9 | 3.6 | 2.2 | 3.8 | −0.7 |
| 1973–79 | 0.5 | 0.2 | −1.4 | 3.1 | 0.3 | 1.9 | −2.6 |

*Source:* J. Kendrick, "International Comparisons of Recent Productivity Trends," in *Essays in Contemporary Economic Problems, Demand, Productivity, and Population,* 1981–82 edition, ed. W. Fellner (Washington, D.C.: American Enterprise Institute for Public Policy Research, 1981), Table 1, p. 128.
*Note:* Data refer to the private (business) sector.

trast with the 1960–73 period, and similar decelerations in productivity across the two periods were observed in each country shown in
Table 17 and in the averages for eight western European countries
(France, West Germany, Italy, United Kingdom, Belgium, Denmark,
the Netherlands, and Sweden). In addition, productivity deteriorated
from 1979 to 1980 for each country shown.

TABLE 16

Rankings of Nine Countries by Percent Changes
in Total Factor Productivity,
1960–73 and 1973–79

| Rank | Country | Total Factor Productivity Percent Change, 1960–73 | Rank | Country | Total Factor Productivity Percent Change, 1973–79 |
|---|---|---|---|---|---|
| 1 | Japan | 6.6 | 1 | Belgium | 2.6 |
| 2 | Italy | 5.8 | 2 | France | 2.1 |
| | | | 2 | West Germany | 2.1 |
| 3 | Belgium | 4.2 | 3 | Japan | 1.8 |
| 4 | France | 3.9 | 4 | Italy | 0.8 |
| 5 | Sweden | 3.6 | 5 | United States | 0.6 |
| 6 | West Germany | 3.2 | 6 | United Kingdom | 0.3 |
| | | | 6 | Sweden | 0.3 |
| 7 | Canada | 2.9 | 7 | Canada | −0.1 |
| 8 | United Kingdom | 2.2 | | | |
| 9 | United States | 1.9 | | | |

Source: Table 15.
Note: Data refer to the private sector.

Hourly compensation in France rose at a rate exceeding the average rate for the eight European nations in each year from 1976 through 1979 (see Table 17); for 1980 the percent increases for the two were equal. The increase in hourly compensation for France in 1980 was the largest among the single years shown for that country and was the third largest among the countries in the table for that year. Some of the effects of inflation can be noted if one compares hourly compensation with real hourly compensation (the latter is obtained by dividing the former by the country's CPI figure for the given year). The increase of 15.0 percent in hourly compensation in France, for example, becomes an increase of 1.3 percent in real terms. Note that real hourly compensation declined in 1980 for four countries (Japan, Sweden, United States, and Canada).

Changes in French unit labor costs, which reflect changes in both productivity and hourly compensation, were above 14 percent for each year from 1978 through 1980, advancing in 1980 at almost three times the rate for 1977 (these costs are expressed in U.S. dollars and thus take account of changes in exchange rates). Moreover, the increase in unit labor costs for 1980 was second only to that of the United Kingdom among the countries shown and was also above the

## TABLE 17

## Output per Hour, Hourly Compensation, and Unit Labor Costs in Manufacturing for Nine Countries, 1960-80
### (Average annual rates of change)

| Country | 1960-73 | 1973-80 | 1976[a] | 1977[a] | 1978[a] | 1979[a] | 1980[a] |
|---|---|---|---|---|---|---|---|
| | | | Output per Hour | | | | |
| France | 6.0 | 4.9 | 8.2 | 5.0 | 5.3 | 5.4 | 0.6 |
| West Germany | 5.5 | 4.8 | 6.4 | 5.3 | 3.8 | 6.3 | -0.7 |
| Japan | 10.7 | 6.8 | 9.4 | 7.2 | 7.9 | 8.0 | 6.2 |
| Belgium | 7.0 | 6.2 | 10.3 | 5.0 | 6.0 | 5.8 | 3.6 |
| Italy | 6.9 | 3.6 | 8.6 | 1.1 | 2.9 | 7.3 | 6.7 |
| Sweden | 6.7 | 2.1 | 1.0 | -1.5 | 4.3 | 8.1 | 0.6 |
| United States | 3.0 | 1.7 | 4.4 | 2.4 | 0.9 | 1.1 | -0.3 |
| Canada | 4.5 | 2.2 | 4.9 | 5.1 | 3.1 | 1.2 | -1.4 |
| United Kingdom | 4.3 | 1.9 | 4.0 | 1.6 | 3.2 | 3.3 | 0.3 |
| 8 European Countries | 5.9 | 4.2 | 7.1 | 3.4 | 4.1 | 5.9 | 2.3 |
| | | | Hourly Compensation | | | | |
| France | 9.7 | 15.2 | 14.3 | 14.1 | 12.9 | 13.9 | 15.0 |
| West Germany | 9.4 | 9.7 | 7.3 | 9.9 | 8.5 | 9.1 | 7.9 |
| Japan | 14.6 | 10.5 | 6.7 | 9.7 | 5.9 | 6.6 | 7.1 |
| Belgium | 10.7 | 12.0 | 12.1 | 11.0 | 7.0 | 7.4 | 10.1 |
| Italy | 12.3 | 20.1 | 19.8 | 18.8 | 14.4 | 17.6 | 21.3 |
| Sweden | 10.1 | 13.8 | 18.0 | 8.6 | 13.5 | 8.4 | 11.1 |
| United States | 5.0 | 9.3 | 8.0 | 8.3 | 8.2 | 9.8 | 10.7 |
| Canada | 6.4 | 11.9 | 14.3 | 12.8 | 7.5 | 9.9 | 9.4 |
| United Kingdom | 8.7 | 19.1 | 17.0 | 11.7 | 16.2 | 19.3 | 23.6 |
| 8 European Countries | 9.9 | 13.8 | 12.7 | 11.7 | 11.6 | 13.0 | 15.0 |
| | | | Real Hourly Compensation[b] | | | | |
| France | 5.1 | 4.2 | 4.2 | 4.3 | 3.5 | 2.9 | 1.3 |
| West Germany | 6.3 | 5.2 | 1.8 | 6.1 | 5.9 | 5.1 | 2.9 |
| Japan | 8.2 | 1.7 | -2.5 | 1.5 | 1.6 | 2.8 | -0.6 |
| Belgium | 6.9 | 3.9 | 2.7 | 3.6 | 2.4 | 2.8 | 3.2 |
| Italy | 7.9 | 2.7 | 2.8 | -0.4 | 1.7 | 1.6 | 0.1 |
| Sweden | 5.3 | 3.3 | 7.0 | -2.6 | 3.2 | 1.1 | -2.3 |
| United States | 1.8 | 0.7 | 2.1 | 1.7 | 0.5 | -1.3 | -2.5 |
| Canada | 3.0 | 2.6 | 6.3 | 4.4 | -1.3 | 0.7 | -0.7 |
| United Kingdom | 3.7 | 3.1 | 0.4 | -3.6 | 7.3 | 5.2 | 4.7 |
| 8 European Countries | 5.7 | 4.0 | 2.9 | 2.0 | 4.6 | 3.9 | 2.8 |

TABLE 17 (continued)

| Country | 1960-73 | 1973-80 | 1976[a] | 1977[a] | 1978[a] | 1979[a] | 1980[a] |
|---|---|---|---|---|---|---|---|
| | | | Unit Labor Costs in U.S. Dollars | | | | |
| France | 2.8 | 10.9 | -5.3 | 5.5 | 17.1 | 14.3 | 15.3 |
| West Germany | 6.1 | 11.2 | -1.6 | 13.1 | 21.0 | 12.4 | 9.8 |
| Japan | 4.9 | 8.3 | -2.4 | 13.3 | 26.2 | -5.7 | -2.5 |
| Belgium | 4.6 | 10.6 | -3.4 | 13.7 | 15.1 | 8.8 | 6.7 |
| Italy | 5.4 | 9.6 | -13.3 | 10.5 | 15.6 | 12.0 | 10.5 |
| Sweden | 4.2 | 11.3 | 11.5 | 8.2 | 5.6 | 5.1 | 12.0 |
| United States | 1.9 | 7.5 | 3.4 | 5.7 | 7.3 | 8.6 | 11.0 |
| Canada | 1.9 | 6.4 | 12.5 | -0.4 | -2.8 | 5.7 | 11.1 |
| United Kingdom | 2.9 | 15.3 | -8.5 | 7.0 | 24.0 | 27.7 | 35.1 |
| 8 European Countries | 4.2 | 11.4 | -5.1 | 9.7 | 18.6 | 14.5 | 14.1 |

*Source:* P. Capdevielle and D. Alvarez, "International Comparisons of Trends in Productivity and Labor Costs," *Monthly Labor Review* (December 1981), Tables 1, 3, and 4.

*Notes:* Rates of change are calculated from the least squares trend of the logarithms of the corresponding index numbers. This is intended to correct for cyclical influences on the average rates of change and provide a better estimate of underlying trend.

All percent changes are calculated from indices, 1977 = 100. Productivity measures do not measure contributions of labor as a separate factor of production but reflect the joint influence of many factors, including new technology, capital investment, capacity utilization, and managerial and labor force skills.

[a] Percent change for a given year is the year-to-year percent change of the corresponding index number.

[b] Real hourly compensation attempts to measure employer expenditures for the benefit of workers. It includes gross pay; bonuses; and employer contributions to insurance programs and welfare plans, pension plans, and medical plans. It is computed by dividing hourly compensation by the consumer price index for each country; thus, real compensation measures are not fully comparable because of differences in definitions of consumer price indices, notably in the cross-country differences in the treatment of owner-occupied housing. See Capdevielle and Alvarez, p. 18, for a discussion of this issue.

eight-country average for this year. The acceleration in unit labor costs appears to be attributable largely to the deterioration in productivity growth in most countries.

Table 18 gives data for France and West Germany. In terms of percent changes in manufacturing output and in output per hour, there is little difference, perhaps surprisingly, between the two countries. Percent changes in productivity (output per hour) in France sometimes exceeded those in West Germany and at other times were exceeded by the latter.

Manufacturing productivity and related measures for France are summarized in Table 19. Percent changes in hours worked (both in

TABLE 18

Output and Output per Hour in Manufacturing and
Percent Change from Year to Year, France and
West Germany, 1975–80

| | France | | | | West Germany | | |
| --- | --- | --- | --- | --- | --- | --- | --- |
| Year | Output | Percent Change | Output per Hour | Percent Change | Output | Percent Change | Output per Hour | Percent Change |
| 1975 | 90.2 | −2.1 | 88.0 | 3.1 | 90.8 | −5.2 | 89.3 | 4.8 |
| 1976 | 96.5 | 6.9 | 95.2 | 8.2 | 97.3 | 7.2 | 95.0 | 6.4 |
| 1977 | 100.0 | 3.6 | 100.0 | 5.0 | 100.0 | 2.8 | 100.0 | 5.3 |
| 1978 | 102.7 | 2.7 | 105.3 | 5.3 | 101.8 | 1.8 | 103.8 | 3.8 |
| 1979 | 106.0 | 3.2 | 111.0 | 5.4 | 106.8 | 4.9 | 110.3 | 6.3 |
| 1980 | 104.8 | −1.1 | 111.7 | 0.6 | 107.2 | 0.4 | 109.5 | −0.7 |

*Source:* Capdevielle and Alvarez, Tables 1, 3, and 4.
*Note:* Output and output per hour are index numbers having base 1977 = 100.

total and in average weekly hours worked) declined in 1980, as did employment, continuing the negative performances that had been observed in each of these variables for each year since 1975. For 1980, output showed a decline; and a substantial portion of the modest productivity gain of 0.6 percent, accomplished despite the large increase in hourly compensation for that year, was accounted for by the decrease in employee hours. Indeed, the gains in productivity and output since 1976 largely reflect significant decreases in labor input throughout this period.

## Industrial Policy

Industrial policy has been debated for nearly 20 years, and although it has given rise to a large literature in many languages, it has not been given a sharp definition; it may be, in fact, that such a definition is impossible to develop. Industrial policy has been referred to as "the notion that governments should do more towards industry than just provide it with a general legal and macro-economic framework."[17] Alternatively, one reads: "Industrial policies will be understood to refer to 'industry-specific' or 'sectoral' policies, notably to direct and indirect subsidies to particular industries or to parts of industries located in particular regions, to voluntary export restraints

17. L. G. Franko, "Industrial Policies in Western Europe – Solution or Problem?," *The World Economy* 2 (1979):31.

TABLE 19

Summary of Annual Percent Changes in Manufacturing
Activity, France, 1975–80

|  | 1975 | 1976 | 1977 | 1978 | 1979 | 1980 |
|---|---|---|---|---|---|---|
| Output per Hour | 3.1 | 8.2 | 5.0 | 5.3 | 5.4 | 0.6 |
| Output | −2.1 | 6.9 | 3.6 | 2.7 | 3.2 | −1.1 |
| Hourly Compensation | 19.7 | 14.3 | 14.1 | 12.9 | 13.9 | 15.0 |
| Real Hourly Compensation | 7.1 | 4.2 | 4.3 | 3.5 | 2.9 | 1.3 |
| Unit Labor Costs in U.S. Dollars | 30.3 | −5.3 | 5.5 | 17.1 | 14.3 | 15.3 |
| Total Hours Worked | −5.0 | −1.1 | −1.3 | −2.4 | −2.2 | −1.7 |
| Average Weekly Hours Worked | −2.3 | −0.1 | −0.9 | −0.7 | −0.4 | −0.3 |
| Employment | −2.7 | −1.0 | −0.5 | −1.7 | −1.8 | −1.4 |

*Source:* Capdevielle and Alvarez, Tables 1, 3, and 4.

negotiated with suppliers of imports, import quotas and tariffs, and to export subsidies and taxes."[18]

Distinctions are also drawn between "positive" industrial policies, which attempt to implement some strategy in a consistent way, and "negative" or "defensive" policies, such as "short-run" attempts to preserve employment in a particular industry or to prevent a greater decline in employment from taking place. Both of these variations usually rely on subsidies and indirect taxes as a principal means of expression.

An example of positive policies is efforts to improve efficiency in an industry. These can be expressed in a variety of ways. Real wages may be taken as a given, but the aim can be "to maintain employment...by pushing up the marginal private and social products of labour, possibly by raising the marginal physical product."[19] Alternatively, the goal may be to "get real wage rates down, at least temporarily, while adjustment measures work themselves out,"[20] or to reduce the labor force in an industry in an orderly way and to minimize dislocations rather than to attempt to preserve employment in defensive ways. On the other hand, defensive policies often involve attempts to keep real labor costs constant in an industry and to provide protection

18. W. M. Corden, "Relationships between Macro-economic and Industrial Policies," *The World Economy* 3 (1980):167; for other discussions of the definition of industrial policy, see Organization for Economic Cooperation and Development, *The Aims and Instruments of Industrial Policy: A Comparative Study* (Paris: OECD, 1975); and J. Pinder, T. Hosomi, and W. Diebold, *Industrial Policy and the International Economy* (New York, Tokyo, and Paris: Trilateral Commission, 1979).

19. Corden, p. 168.

20. Ibid.

or subsid es to make an industry "privately, though not socially, economic "21

In trying to understand what industrial policies are, the question naturally arises: how does one distinguish between them and the standard macroeconomic policies of government? One might believe, as the comments above suggest, that the latter influence the general level of economic activity, whereas industrial policies are designed to influence particular industries. This separation breaks down very quickly, however, as a moment's reflection will indicate. Most macroeconomic policies have industry-specific ramifications; likewise, industrial policies can influence macroeconomic policies and in this way have ramifications beyond the industry. An example of the latter would be efforts to increase employment in an industry which turn out to be successful, thus increasing total employment somewhat. This, in turn, could influence policymakers by reducing pressures on them to take actions to reduce unemployment. A problem with industrial policy occurs, obviously, with the reversing of this sequence: monetary authorities may be forced to adopt a tight monetary policy which, in turn, has unfavorable effects upon employment in an industry; political demands are then created for an industrial policy to bail out the affected industry. Unfortunately, neither governments nor taxpayers seem to be adequately aware that the preservation of employment in a given industry is often paid for by taking real resources away from other industrial sectors which may be in good health, or rom individual taxpayers, or both. Healthy firms may thus be taxed — either directly or indirectly by a reduction in the demand for their output as a result of taxes that individuals pay — causing their employment-generating capabilities to be reduced. It is a melancholy truism that the trade-offs involved in subsidies, whether part of an industrial policy or not, are rarely analyzed and understood by the public.

France is regarded as the first Western practitioner of industrial policy in the post-World War II period, and for many years it has employed an extensive collection of government devices to influence industries. These have included:

(a) fostering infant industries and technology, especially those related to military or energy security;

(b) up-grading technology and productivity; and promoting the exploitation of economies of scale in existing industries, especially to prepare these industries for the dramatic reduction in tariff and quota protection against foreign competition which the French Government also accepted after 1958;

21. Ibid., p. 70.

(c) maintaining (or obtaining) national ownership in industries deemed vulnerable to foreign exercise of economic or political monopoly power;

(d) influencing industry or economy-wide wage settlements and labour relations by "model" bargains (wage bargains in the government-owned Renault Company were often entered with this leadership role in mind);

(e) dispersing industrial activity to depressed or under-developed regions;

(f) underpinning particular firms whose skills and resources were deemed long-term national assets, with extraordinary credit infusions during cyclical dips in demand (or during spells of real or perceived foreign "predatory" competition);

(g) promoting the mobility of workers and capital across industries and among regions; and even

(h) obliging firms to introduce "socially useful" products (as when, shortly after World War II, the Government ordered Renault to introduce its "people's car," the 4-cv).[22]

An important feature of French industrial policy "was to follow no rigid 'market' versus 'non-market' approaches to economic management, but rather to support, strengthen, salvage, and promote industry on a selective basis."[23] Whatever may be the truth of this, Table 20 summarizes the major types of industrial policies employed in France by the middle of the 1970s.

With respect to developments since 1976, the attitudes and efforts of the Barre program vis-à-vis industrial policy were not, as we have noted earlier, consistent with other aspects of its private enterprise policies. Although the Barre program did deal with some lame duck industries (notably in textiles and steel) in ways which differed from the protectionism of the past, it moved ahead with government intervention in selected high-technology businesses, largely by providing subsidies and encouraging merger activities. Important examples were: (1) the merger of St. Gobain-Pont-à-Mousson with Olivetti (an Italian firm), which also provided a link between these firms and CII-Honeywell Bull, a 10 percent share of which is owned by St. Gobain; (2) government aid to a collection of small software companies working for France's five major electronic firms (Thomson-CSF, CII-Honeywell Bull, St. Gobain-Pont-à-Mousson, CIT-Alcatel, and Matra); and (3) expansion of government aid and ownership share in a large variety of energy activities and defense-related businesses.

Other nations, by no means limited to the Western world, have also embraced industrial policies since the mid-1960s. West Germany and the United States have developed policies to promote high-technology

22. Franko, p. 33. A detailed discussion of industrial policies employed by France in the 1960s is given in L. Stoléru, *L'Impératif industriel* (Paris: Editions du Seuil, 1969).
23. Franko, pp. 33–34.

TABLE 20

A Classification of Industrial Policies in France in the Mid-1970s

| Sector or Activity | Direct Subsidies or Tax Relief | Credit Allocations | National Procurement Preferences | Merger Promotions | Nationalization | Rationalization Arguments, Cartels, etc. |
|---|---|---|---|---|---|---|
| Textiles | | X | | X | | |
| Oil | X | X | | X | | |
| Coal | X | | | X | | X |
| Nuclear Power | X | X | X | X | X | X |
| Steel | X | X | | X | | |
| Shipbuilding | X | X | | X | | |
| Aircraft | X | X | X | X | X | |
| Automobiles | X | | | X | | |
| Vehicle Components | | | | X | | |
| Electronic Components | | X | X | | | |
| Computers | X | | X | X | X (Partial) | |
| Telecommunications | | | X | X | X | |
| Food Processing | | | | X | | |
| Regional Aids | X | X | | X | | |
| Export Promotion | X | X | | | | |

Source: L. G. Franko, "Industrial Policies in Western Europe—Solution or Problem?," The World Economy 2 (1979), Table 1, p. 42.

sectors such as the aerospace industry, computers, and nuclear energy, especially where the required investments are large and national defense implications are present.[24] Industrial policies in Britain have included the promotion of mergers, the subsidization of declining industries (notably the steel industry), and the blocking of takeovers of British firms by foreign corporations. Industrial policies have also been pursued in Belgium, the Netherlands, Italy, Sweden, South Korea, and extensively in Japan. In various nations industrial policies have been closely related to national planning activities, and in France some of the industrial policies have been developed through the Commissariat du plan, the government organization directly concerned with planning in France.

Although the aims of industrial policies are often stated in terms of developing new industries so as to improve employment and a country's ability to compete more effectively in the international economy, most of the subsidies engendered by these policies have been given to assist mature industries in various states of decline, rather than to promote industries whose future growth prospects might be regarded as favorable.[25] Indeed, in most countries government assistance to new, high-technology industries has been a small proportion of that going to aging industries in economic difficulty. This has been particularly true in France; as Berger has stated:

> . . . what is striking in the French case is that government is retreating from the sectors and activities that are likely to grow, while increasing its involvement in declining sectors. That it calls the former economic liberalism and the latter social intervention may matter little for the political result. What kinds of successes can the government hope for with no more direct strategy for defending employment than industrial rescue operations? . . . What kind of successes can government survive, when it engages its resources and prestige to prop up industries whose preservation may be as problematic as their demise?[26]

Although industrial policy has many supporters and its use in many nations continues to expand, numerous doubts concerning its employment exist. These largely relate to the unintended economic effects of extending industrial policy beyond the favored industry,

24. For a consideration of industrial policy in West Germany, see J. B. Donges, "Industrial Policies in West Germany's Not So Market-oriented Economy," *The World Economy* 3 (1980):185–94.
25. Franko, pp. 41–45; G. de Carmoy, "Subsidy Policies in Britain, France, and West Germany: An Overview," in *International Trade and Industrial Policies,* ed. S. Warnecke (New York: Holmes & Meier Publishers, 1978), pp. 35–57. See also J. Zysman, *Political Strategies for Industrial Order: State, Market and Industry in France* (Berkeley, Cal.: University of California Press, 1977); and G. Ohlin, "Subsidies and Other Industrial Aids," in Warnecke, pp. 21–34.
26. Berger, pp. 307–8.

and to the inevitable, continuing, and gargantuan problems of political implementation. A good statement summarizing these two classes
of problems is the following:

> Technically it is perfectly possible to devise a policy that assists an indus-
> try temporarily, possibly with an automatically declining rate of protection
> built into the initial arrangements. But in practice it is possible to think of
> many examples where protection was originally imposed because of a
> short-term decline and where the protection stayed on even when the
> urgent need has disappeared. For example, in Western Europe (other than
> Britain) agricultural protectionism was given its first big boost in the agri-
> cultural depression of the 1870s, and the consequences are still with us.
>
> Apart from the question as to whether the possibly favorable effects of
> short-term protection would not be outweighed by the long-term adverse
> effects when the protection is inevitably not temporary, there is also the
> more fundamental issue as to whether "made to measure intervention"
> involving many detailed micro-decisions is desirable. . . . Given sufficient
> information, there may exist in theory an "optimal" system of intervention,
> but will the political process produce it? May it not produce a socially non-
> optimal set of interventions, responsive to pressure groups and imposing
> extra costs through its complexity?[27]

Corden has raised the question of whether made-to measure intervention, with its many firm-level decisions, is desirable; a deeper
question is whether such intervention can be brought about efficiently on a consistent basis. To put it another way and somewhat
more bluntly, can industrial policy as practiced in France and some
other countries, where the government is so heavily involved, be
other than futile? It may well be the case that industrial policies have
failed not so much because there have not been genuine attempts to
implement them, but because effective implementation is impossible,
even apart from the political problems that Corden and others have
mentioned.

It seems to be very easy to say – as supporters of industrial policy
have – that the government can become more selective in its interventions; but it is very difficult to define in operational terms just what
this means. Furthermore, it appears to be very difficult to establish
performance criteria for any governmental agency by reference to
which it can evaluate the efficiency of its own interventions in the
economy. To do this, an agency must come to grips with the vast
problem of assessing the costs and anticipated benefits of a given
intervention and comparing these with the costs and anticipated
benefits of alternate interventions that might be contemplated.

The enormous operational difficulty of these problems can be made
clearer by means of a specific example from current French industrial

27. Corden, p. 177.

policy. The government is heavily involved with several industries in developing Télématique, the name given to the business of marketing computer terminals which will be used in offices and homes and linked by telephone lines to large-scale computers. This is a high-priority government project involving merger activities between the Saint-Gobain-Pont-à-Mousson group and Olivetti, which we have already noted, and a variety of other partnership arrangements with the government. Télématique falls into the class of high-technology industries whose development President Giscard d'Estaing was on record for supporting vigorously. An important feature of this new business is the government-owned telephone monopoly which will be, of course, a basic part of the enterprise because users will access central computers by means of it.[28]

Many difficult questions arise in connection with the government's decision to intervene in such activities. Such questions are related to market research and the production and sale of a complex product which may undergo rapid technological development even before the system is operational. What are the anticipated markets for this business? What are the expected market shares? What is the expected return on the government's investment? Will the market expand rapidly enough so that rising output will permit lowering of prices and the gaining of a strong competitive position? What are the trade-offs between expected long-run market performance and short-run financial performance, particularly when the latter involves large cash drains which are typical of ventures in high-technology industries? What will be the policies of the other major French competitors and of giant firms headquartered in other countries, such as IBM, Rank-Xerox, and Exxon? Because industrial policy often leads to entry into oligopolies, as is the case with Télématique, or into businesses that may become oligopolies, what might be the reactions of existing firms either in France or in other countries to prevent a new entrant from achieving output levels or a price structure needed to survive without unduly large losses?

The point is that all these questions are extremely difficult to answer, even for specialist firms such as IBM and Rank-Xerox operating as private organizations. How are these and other questions to be answered when, in addition to the usual strategic business management problems, one must consider the peculiar political problems brought about by government partnership, industrial policy, and

---

28. It is interesting to note that the government has plans to exploit this monopoly position by encouraging (coercing?) subscribers to use Télématique to acquire information ordinarily found in conventional paper telephone directories: it recently announced a very large increase in the price of the latter.

government decision making? Although one hears a good deal about these matters in many countries today, the fact remains that we have done very little to conceptualize the problems posed by government partnerships and the mergers, acquisitions, and so on, which often ensue. There is, it must be stressed, no comprehensive and empirically validated theory for dealing with these problems. Such a theory would have to begin by combining satisfactorily at least three disciplines – marketing, business policy, and industrial organization economics – and these have not yet been integrated effectively even in the simpler context of the operations of private firms.

The complexity of these matters may be suggested by Figure 3, which displays some of the major analytical issues relating to a *given* partnership undertaking. To be a "good" government partner or, more generally, to have a "good" industrial policy, one would have to traverse efficiently an analytical framework such as that outlined in Figure 3 for a variety of alternative intervention possibilities and choose a "best" set of partnerships or interventions relative to agreed-upon economic and political criteria. This prospect appears to be prohibitively difficult; it seems that it would be far wiser for governments to reduce their partnership and intervention efforts and to work instead towards freeing markets and encouraging private enterprise to deal with such questions in the context of competition among private firms. The latter are far better equipped to deal with problems of decision making, strategy selection, and risk conceptualization and management arising from their own development and growth requirements than are governments intervening selectively and operating under the usual problems and conflicts of political organizations.

Corden sums up the situation persuasively:

> The term "industrial policy" turns out to some extent to be a euphemism for defensive protection – for policies that shelter industries or regions from adverse changes. . . . There are few, if any, arguments for protection that can stand up as long-term arguments from a national efficiency point of view. Mostly the best industrial policy may be to provide an adequate infrastructure, some limits on the powers of monopolies and cartels, an education system that helps to generate the human capital for industrial success, indicative guidance about industrial prospects (without compulsion or subsidies), stability and simplicity in the system of taxation, a free and flexible capital market and a steady movement towards zero sectional protection, whether direct or indirect. . . . The best industrial policy may well be one that gradually ensures its own disappearance.[29]

## The Continuing Decline of French Planning

Eight national plans of varying degrees of comprehensiveness were developed in France during the period 1946–80. The first of these,

29. Corden, pp. 182–83.

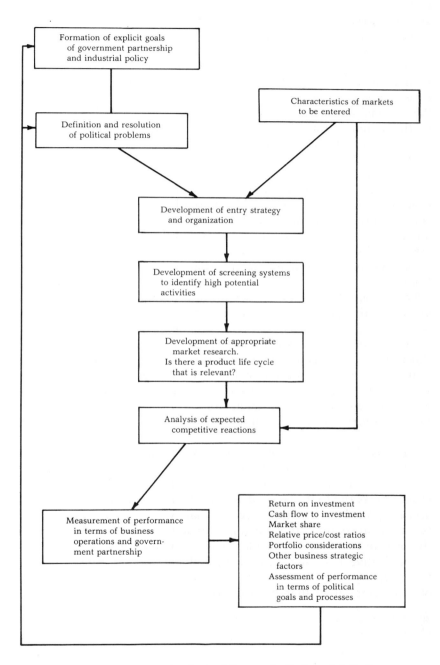

**Figure 3.    Some Analytical Issues in Industrial Policy**

called the Plan de modernization et d'équipement, was drawn up in 1946 by the postliberation government of General de Gaulle and was associated with Jean Monnet. Developed for the period 1947–50, it was subsequently extended to 1952–53 to allow incorporation of Marshall Plan aid and other aspects of the Economic Recovery Plan of the United States. The plan addressed six basic sectors (which were regarded as bottlenecks); it consisted largely of investment plans for the nationalized industries (which had been considerably augmented by the nationalizations of 1945–46); and it led to an important, probably unplanned, result which was to become characteristic of the post-World War II French economy: the extension of the state's direction of investment. This, together with the large and growing mass of public investment required by the nationalized enterprises, led in time to "crowding out" problems, as public and private investment competed with each other and aggregate investment demand continually bumped up against the total levels that the economy could generate, given its interest rate policies and balance of payments problems. This issue, already touched upon earlier, will be considered again in Chapter 3.

The second plan (1954–57) sought to program sustained economic growth. Although it was termed a plan for the entire economy, in contrast to a plan for basic sectors, emphasis on basic sectors and nationalized enterprises continued to have central importance. The third plan (1958–61) also emphasized economic growth but in addition aspired to integrate this with the pursuit of domestic monetary stability and a return to balance of payments equilibrium. The latter was regarded as a breakthrough: for the first time an attempt was made to relate domestic planning to the realities of the international economy.

The fourth plan (1962–65), regarded by many as the high-water mark of French planning, inaugurated several new developments in national planning. It contained very detailed physical output projections, it was the first plan to deal with regional assistance programs, and it applied on a national scale what was referred to as market research procedures, these being intended to reduce uncertainty in the private economy.[30] This plan was celebrated for what was called its "indicative planning" procedures, which were intended to guide the economy towards the attainment of various objectives by means of incentives rather than by administrative directives (called, in con-

30. D. Liggins, "What Can We Learn from French Planning?," *Lloyd's Bank Review* 12 (April 1976):3.

trast, "imperative planning"). The fourth plan also gave extensive emphasis to medium-term objectives and procedures.

Another interesting feature of the fourth plan was that it became widely known and widely discussed, in France and elsewhere, in contrast to previous plans. General de Gaulle, who was again in power by the time this plan was being prepared, gave the fourth plan strong support in a major speech (May 1961), in which he referred to *"l'ardente obligation du Plan"* and exhorted his listeners to make the plan into *"la grande affaire de la France."*[31]

The process of consensus building (*concertation*), a feature of French planning from the beginning, became ever more important as the organizational scope of the plans grew larger and larger. Government administrators, businessmen, labor union officials, consultants from universities, and others formed commissions, councils, committees, and working parties to discuss various aspects of the plans, including the reconciliation of objectives (a process called consistency). This *concertation* process reached gargantuan proportions in a relatively short time; a prominent official in the French planning apparatus has said that there were about 4,000 such commissions, committees, and satellite organizations in 1960, the totality of which was referred to as the "consultative administration."[32]

The fifth plan (1966–70) was similar to the fourth in many respects but assigned fundamental importance to strengthening the productive sectors of the economy and extended regional development goals. There was also a nonmandatory incomes policy; goals were stated in monetary terms rather than in physical output terms; and the role of government was larger while that of business was smaller than in previous plans.[33] A principal theme of the plan was to prepare France for effective competition with its EEC partners.

The sixth plan (1971–75) moved still further in the direction of a "government plan"—one in which the government plays a dominant role. The seventh plan was developed for the period 1976–79 and the eighth for 1980–85. Supporters of national planning have raised ques-

31. Cited in V. C. Lutz, *French Planning* (Washington: American Enterprise Institute for Public Policy Research, 1965), p. 3.

32. J.-J. Bonnaud, "Planning and Industry in France," in *Planning, Politics, and Public Policy,* ed. J. Hayward and M. Watson (London: Cambridge University Press, 1975), p. 94. Bonnaud also stresses that close affinities exist between the plans and industrial policy. See also B. Molitor, "Politique industrielle et planification en France," *Revue économique* 31 (September 1980):837–52.

33. J. H. McArthur and B. R. Scott, *Industrial Planning in France* (Boston: Harvard Graduate School of Business Administration, 1969), pp. 43–44.

tions about the seventh and eighth plans; one writer has claimed that they demonstrate that French planning has been "steadily emptied of content (over and above the budgeting of a limited number of medium-term actions)."[34] This writer also complained that the eighth plan "threatens to be a further stage in the 'unplanning' of National Planning," and concluded that, with it, "'democratic planning' (in the shape of consensus building) is gradually and explicitly being replaced – if indeed it ever existed – by 'technocratic planning' (in the shape of medium-term budgeting)."[35] The eighth plan retreated further from the pattern set by previous plans by failing to include normative forecasts of future values. These were omitted because it was believed that uncertainties in the international economy made it pointless to attempt to quantify future economic prospects. It appears, moreover, that the Barre program and its goals of controlling inflation, stabilizing the franc, and so on (see first section of this chapter) in effect took precedence over both the seventh and eighth plans, thus confirming the pessimistic assessments of planning advocates. The seventh plan was apparently used largely for medium-term budgetary management of public investment projects, and this appears to have been the chief use of the eighth plan as well, at least while the Barre administration was in office.

In any case, planning activities since 1970 have engaged the efforts of smaller numbers of committees, commissions, and individuals. In contrast to the approximately 4,000 commissions reportedly working on the fourth plan, the sixth plan had 26 commissions, the seventh had 13, and the eighth had 7 commissions and 7 committees.[36]

Many students of French planning assert that its decline began shortly after the inception of the fourth plan in the early 1960s. Although this plan had been the country's most elaborate and comprehensive up to that time, it quickly ran into difficulties because of increasing inflation and rapidly growing balance of payments problems – which had not been anticipated and hence were not accommodated in the plan. Each of the French plans, in fact, was concerned with "end point" goals and objectives (usually stated in the form of forecasts of desired levels of selected variables for the final year of the planning period), and failed to provide – indeed, probably could not provide – either specification of "desirable" paths to traverse toward the goals or alternative possibilities to pursue if major

34. D. Green, "The Budget and the Plan," in *French Politics and Public Policy,* ed P. G. Cerny and M. A. Schain (New York: St. Martin's Press, 1980), p. 120.

35. Ibid.

36. Ibid., p. 124. See also D. Green, "The Seventh Plan – The Demise of French Planning?," *West European Politics* 1 (February 1978):60-70.

unanticipated economic or social developments were to intrude during the period of the plan.[37] The fourth plan had to be interrupted in 1963 and was essentially replaced by an economic "package" called the Stabilization Plan (which was not a plan at all) put forth by the finance minister at the time, Giscard d'Estaing. The fifth plan was abandoned after the events of May 1968 (could these have been foreseen in 1965?) and the sixth plan was rendered irrelevant by the oil and commodity crisis of 1973–74 (again, could this have been anticipated in 1970?), to which the government responded with a sequence of moves developed without regard to the plan. Whether the decline in French planning since the early 1960s is attributable to changing interests, enthusiasms, and deliberate attenuation efforts of successive presidents and their associates, or to international influences and administrative arrangements emanating from membership in the EEC, or to still other economic developments within or outside France, or to some combination of all of these, remains an interesting and unresolved question.[38]

## Notes on Chapter 2

An excellent treatment of the economic policies of post-1973 France, which gives attention also to the oil shock and subsequent energy problems in France, is A. Cotta's *La France et l'impératif mondial* (Paris: Presses universitaires de France, 1978). The same author has also written an informative study of inflation in France since 1962, *Inflation et croissance en France depuis 1962* (Paris: Presses

37. There is a serious and profound question whether a national planning apparatus can deal with such contingencies and with the enormous complexities of developing alternative adjustments, even if accurate forecasts could be developed (and this is highly unlikely, as is attested to by the many unhappy forecasts in the West for periods of more than two years ahead, particularly in the 1970s). The liberal (in the European sense) view holds that the private economy, with its system of firm and industry adjustment procedures and its mix of individual responsibilities and decisions (augmented by "appropriate" macroeconomic policies on the part of government) is an inherently superior means for dealing with these challenges. An articulate statement of this view is M. Friedman's *Market Mechanisms and Central Economic Planning*, the Second G. Warren Nutter Lecture given at the Hoover Institution, March 4, 1981 (Washington, D.C.: American Enterprise Institute for Public Policy Research, 1981). Others hold that national plans are inevitably too inflexible and that the increasing dynamism and "shock" potential of the international economy make elaborate national plans increasingly inapplicable.
38. J. Delors, using a broad brush, attributes the decline of French planning to economic, social, and political problems. See his paper, "The Decline of French Planning," in *Beyond Capitalist Planning*, ed. S. Holland (New York: St. Martin's Press, 1979), pp. 9–33.

universitaires de France, 1974). Still another study, available in English, is J. Marczewski's, *Inflation and Unemployment in France* (New York: Praeger Publishers, 1978). A good survey of economic developments in the period 1958–78 is B. Belassa's "The French Economy under the Fifth Republic, 1958–78," in *The Fifth Republic at Twenty*, edited by W. G. Andrews and S. Hoffmann (Albany: State University of New York Press, 1981):204–26.

Two excellent references on energy problems in France are *Energy for Europe: Political Implications*, by Guy de Carmoy (Washington: American Enterprise Institute for Public Policy Research, 1977), and "Energy Policies of the Fifth Republic: Autonomy Versus Constraint," by R. J. Lieber, in *The Fifth Republic at Twenty*, op. cit. The latter is particularly good on political aspects of energy policies. Alain Cances, in *Les Petrodollars en France* (Paris: Editions Fayolle, 1978), examines economic implications of "petrodollars" and other aspects of the energy problem with respect to France.

Further information on problems of unemployment can be found in a paper by R. T. Kaufman, "Patterns of Unemployment in North America, Western Europe and Japan," in *Unemployment in Western Countries*, proceedings of a conference held by the International Economic Association at Bischenburg, France, and edited by E. Malinvaud and J.-P. Fitoussi (London: Macmillan Press, Ltd., 1980):3–35. An interesting theoretical examination of the relationship between unemployment and labor costs is S. Nickell's "Unemployment and the Structure of Labor Costs," in *Policies for Employment, Prices, and Exchange Rates*, edited by K. Brunner and A. H. Meltzer (Amsterdam: North-Holland Publishing Co., 1979):187–222. W. W. Daniel and E. Stilgoe study the economic effects of legislation intended to protect employed workers in *The Impact of Employment Protection Laws* (London: Policies Studies Institute, 1978). Problems of technical change, employment, and inflation in European countries, including France, are examined in an OECD publication, *Technical Change and Economic Policy* (Paris: OECD, 1980). A good survey of productivity problems in advanced economies is "The Slowdown of Productivity Growth: Some Contributing Factors," by J. R. Norsworthy, M. J. Harper, and K. Kunze, *Brookings Papers on Economic Activity* 2 (1979):387–421. Two views of inflation can be found in *Curing Chronic Inflation*, by A. Okun and G. L. Perry (Washington: The Brookings Institution, 1978), and "New Policies to Fight Inflation: Sources of Skepticism," by A. Rees, *Brookings Papers on Economic Activity* 2 (1978):453–77. D. J. B. Mitchell studies the relation between wage rates, unionization, and inflation in *Wages, Unions and Inflation* (Washington: The Brookings Institution, 1980).

There is a large literature on the economics of minimum wages. Two excellent treatments of basic issues are "Impact of Minimum Wages on Other Wages, Employment, and Family Incomes," by E. M. Gramlich, *Brookings Papers on Economic Activity* 2 (Washington: Brookings Institution, 1976):409–51, and "The Effects of Minimum Wages on the Distribution of Changes in Aggregate Employment," by M. Kosters and F. Welch, *American Economic Review* 62 (June 1972):323–32. Another good study is F. Welch and J. Cunningham's "Effects of Minimum Wages on the Level and Age Composition of Youth Employment," *Review of Economics and Statistics* 60 (February 1978):140–45.

The industrial policies of France prior to 1973 are discussed in an OECD publication, *The Industrial Policy of France* (Paris: OECD, 1974), and also in Y. Ullmo's "France," in *Planning, Politics, and Public Policy*, edited by J. Hayward and M. Watson (London: Cambridge University Press, 1975):22–51. Good surveys of French planning are those by J. Fourastié, *La Planification en France* (Paris: Presses universitaires de France, 1968); C. P. Kindleberger, "French Planning," in *National Economic Planning*, edited by M. F. Millikan (New York: Columbia University Press, 1967):279–303; and D. Liggins, *National Economic Planning in France* (Lexington, Mass.: Lexington Books, 1975). The latter provides a good treatment of the sixth plan and its various underlying economic models, and of the large-scale econometric model used to make forecasts (called the "medium-term physico-financial projection model" and given the acronym FIFI); an appendix contains a good summary of the first four plans. J.-J. Carré, P. Dubois, and E. Malinvaud have written a thorough study of French planning which is guardedly approving: *La Croissance française: un essai d'analyse économique causale de l'après-guerre* (Paris: Editions du Seuil, 1972). An English translation is available under the title *French Economic Growth* (Stanford, Cal.: Stanford University Press, 1975). Economic interrelationships between French planning and common market policies are illuminatingly examined in B. Belassa's "Planning and Programming in the European Common Market," *European Economic Review* 8 (1973):217–33.

Planning in many Western nations has collided with the realities of budgeting and hence with the powers of bureaucracies; a study of these issues is "The Budget and the Plan in France," by J. Carassus, in *Planning in Europe*, edited by J. Hayward and O. Narkiewicz (London: Croom Helm, 1978):53–66. Largely concerned with the seventh plan, this article examines RBOs (rationalization of budget options) and PAPs (priority action programs). The role and accuracy of forecasts in various French plans are examined in an article by S. Estrin and P. M.

Holmes, "The Performance of French Planning 1952–78," *Economics of Planning* 16 (1980):1–19. J. Leruz gives useful comparative comments on planning in "Macro-economic Planning in Mixed Economies: The French and British Experience," in *Planning in Europe,* op. cit.

A sharply unfavorable critique of French planning is S. J. Koch's "Non-Democratic Non-Planning: The French Experience," *Policy Science* 7 (1976):371–85. Calling the sixth plan a major victory for the skeptics (p. 385), she asserts that an analysis of the plans as developed and executed reveals that they "did not meet the standards either of democracy or planning" (p. 371). From the opposite end of the spectrum, J. Attali expresses a desire for a new kind of planning in France, which would be neither managed by private enterprise nor operated centrally by the state in the old ways, but "decentralized in its preparation but strong in its execution," and which would be unified in operation yet antiorganizational in its effects. This would be accomplished, apparently, by expanding state ownership of firms whose management would remain in some way independent, efficient, and decentralized and which would also have, beyond this, increased worker participation in management policy formation (*autogestion*). Perilously close to believing that it is possible to be both centralized and decentralized at the same time, Attali sets forth these desires, fervently, in "Towards Socialist Planning," in *Beyond Capitalist Planning,* edited by S. Holland (New York: St. Martin's Press, 1979), but gives no documentation as to whether such goals can be realized. This is mentioned here because the Mitterand government embarked on a large nationalization scheme shortly after assuming office, and it appears that such views may be tried as an alternative, or at least as an extensive supplement, to the planning mechanisms previously developed in France.

# 3

## Three Key Aspects in Detail:
Monetary, Fiscal, and Balance of Payments Policies

### Overview of the French Financial System

Some knowledge of the financial system and of the operation of money markets in France is necessary to understand important aspects of monetary policy, or even features of a policy mix in which monetary policy is an important component. Unfortunately for the general reader, the French financial system – a unique product of history, economics, and political life – is complex, and few up-to-date summaries of any kind are available in English. Many of the standard references in French are either filled with descriptive detail or give substantial consideration to the theory of finance or other aspects of economic theory, and usually give scant attention to monetary policy and its impacts on the economy. The principal purpose of this section is to provide a brief, nontechnical treatment of the financial system and its more important institutional and operational features, followed by a consideration of monetary policy in the period 1975 to 1981.

The government has extensive influence over financial affairs in France. It expresses this influence not only in the usual ways, through the issuing of currency and government bonds, but also through its governance of the complex layers of financial intermediaries over which it has regulatory powers of various kinds and many of which it owns outright.[1] The government administers the level of interest rates on the money market and thus influences the total volume of savings and available financing; it can allocate funds between various important sectors of the economy and it has the right to appoint the top managers of key financial institutions, whether or not these are owned by the state. In contrast to some other Western nations, notably the United States, West Germany, and Great Britain, there is no tradition of central bank independence; the Treasury's influence on the Banque de France is strong, particularly with respect to issues of monetary policy. Open market operations of the kind employed in the United States are essentially unutilized as a monetary policy tool.

1. Roughly speaking, an intermediary is an institution which stands between economic units having means of financing and those which desire financing.

The primary market for financial instruments is strong and well developed, but the secondary market is weak and poorly developed. Although the structure of the financial system has been evolving slowly for many years, it has been influenced in important ways by relatively recent developments: the banking acts of 1941 and 1945, the Debré reforms of 1966–67, and the Marjolin-Sadrin-Wormser reforms of 1971. The Debré reforms are regarded as having been influential in encouraging the rapid growth of branch banking in France, in transforming the maturity structure of bank assets, and in stimulating the growth of foreign banks operating in France (which doubled in number during the period from 1966 to 1975), while at the same time serving to increase concentration in French banking.[2] These reforms also led to the creation of a mortgage market in France. The American reader, habituated to a well-developed market in which mortgages with 20- to 30-year terms have been common for many years, may be surprised to learn that prior to 1966 a house or apartment buyer in France could get at most a 5-year loan that could be renewed at most one time only. Currently, the maximum term for a mortgage is 16 to 17 years for all but a small number of persons having very high credit ratings.

The most important financial institutions in France can be classified into the following: (1) the registered banks, (2) the savings banks (*caisses d'épargne*), (3) the cooperative banks (*caisses mutuelles*), (4) the system of popular banks, (5) the postal checking system, and (6) the French Bank for Foreign Commerce, or Banque française du commerce extérieur (BFCE).[3]

The registered banks, so called because they are required by law to register with the Conseil national du crédit, number about 380 and are of two kinds: deposit banks (*banques des dépôts*) and merchant banks (*banques des affaires*). The distinctions between these two kinds of banks, delineated by the banking act of 1945, have become less important since the Debré reforms, and many of the latter banks have been absorbed by the former. The deposit banks are dominated by the three large nationalized banks, the Banque nationale de Paris, the

2. B. T. Bayliss and A. A. S. Butt Philip, *Capital Markets and Industrial Investment in Germany and France* (Westmead, England: Saxon House, 1980), p. 136.

3. The discussion in this and the next two sections draws extensively on the excellent treatment in J. Mélitz, *The French Financial System: Mechanisms and Propositions of Reform* (Paris: Institut national de la statistique et des études économiques, 1980). This is the best source available in English; unfortunately it is a working paper (*document de travail*) of INSEE and has been given only a very limited distribution. Descriptive comments on the French money markets and banking system can be found in *Banking Structures and Sources of Finance in the European Community*, 3d ed. (London: Banker Research Unit, 1979), chap. 2; and in *Banking Systems Abroad* (London: Inter-Bank Research Organization, 1978), chap. 3.

Crédit lyonnais, and the Société générale, which together account for about 50 percent of all deposits in registered banks. The savings banks accept only savings accounts and offer no checking account facilities. The cooperative banks have both savings and checking deposits and were originally established to serve the rural population, although they are not so confined today and can be found in cities and other areas. Most of the cooperative banks are affiliated with the national agricultural bank (*Caisse nationale de crédit agricole*, or CNCA). The CNCA is the largest bank in France and by some measures the third largest bank in the world. Anyone can have a savings or a checking account with this bank but it can lend only to customers living in rural areas or engaged in agricultural or related activities. The popular banks originally specialized in serving small businessmen and artisans but have extended their activities beyond these groups and are now found throughout the country. The postal checking system offers facilities for checking accounts only, and the BFCE is concerned with activities having a focus outside France (principally with the promotion of the export business).[4]

Mention should be made of the financial role of the insurance business and of the three types of investment funds, the most important of which is the collection of mutual funds, *sociétés d'investissement à capital variable*, or SICAVs. The insurance business is an unimportant component of the French financial system, the total assets of general and life insurance companies being about 12 percent of those of commercial banks. Nonetheless, the influence of the government in this business is also extensive; it owns eight insurance companies, including the three largest in France. In addition, all other insurance companies are subject to government control over their investment portfolios. The mutual funds, or SICAVs, of which there are about 110 at this writing, are a relatively new component in the financial system, having been approved by the government in the early 1960s. They have since experienced a rapid growth, but they still account for only about 2 percent of the total liabilities and claims of the French financial system.[5] Apparently, the structure and role of the French social security system and the long-standing preference of many French savers for high liquidity are important forces restraining insurance companies and investment trusts to their present relatively unimportant positions. The distributions of deposit shares and of loan shares by major type of financial institution, including the Banque de France, SICAVs, insurance companies, and others, as of the end of 1975, are shown in Tables 21 and 22.

4. Mélitz, p. 4.
5. Bayliss and Butt Philip, p. 145.

## TABLE 21

### Shares of Deposits and Other Liabilities to the Nonfinancial Sector at the End of 1975

| Institution | Billions of French Francs | Percent |
|---|---|---|
| *Central Bank (8.3%)* | | |
| Banque de France | 103.7 | 8.3 |
| *Deposit-Taking Institutions (71.7%)* | | |
| National Banks | 225.8 | 18.1 |
| Other Deposit Banks | 129.9 | 10.4 |
| Investment Banks | 13.1 | 1.1 |
| Popular Banks | 35.8 | 2.9 |
| Agricultural Credit Banks | 147.9 | 11.9 |
| Mutual Credit Banks | 28.0 | 2.2 |
| National Savings Bank | 84.6 | 6.8 |
| Ordinary Savings Banks | 177.5 | 14.2 |
| Post Office Savings | 51.5 | 4.1 |
| *Long-Term Credit Institutions (8.2%)* | | |
| Long-Term Credit Banks | 1.8 | 0.1 |
| Foreign Trade Bank | 2.8 | 0.2 |
| Crédit National | – | – |
| Crédit Foncier | 2.0 | 0.2 |
| Caisse des Dépots et Consignations | 48.3 | 3.9 |
| Other Special Credit Institutions | 3.9 | 0.3 |
| Treasury and Fonds de Développement Economique et Social | 43.3 | 3.5 |
| *Investing Institutions (11.3%)* | | |
| Insurance Companies | 109.2 | 8.8 |
| Mutual Funds (SICAVs) | 25.0 | 2.0 |
| Common Investment Funds | 6.0 | 0.5 |
| *Other Financial Institutions (0.5%)* | | |
| Cooperative Credit Institutions | 1.5 | 0.1 |
| Finance Companies | 4.9 | 0.4 |
| | 1,246.5 | 100.0 |
| Nominal Value of Bonds Outstanding | 229.4 | |
| Market Value of Listed Equities | 163.0 | |

*Source: Banking Systems Abroad* (London: Interbank Research Organization, 1978), Table 7, p. 128.

Equity financing (i.e., financing by means of the stock market), an important feature of financial markets in many Western countries, is relatively undersized in France, although rigorous efforts have been made by the government since 1977 to encourage its growth. The Loi Monory, passed in 1978, allows a personal income tax deduction of up to 5,000 francs each year until 1982 for new investments in French

TABLE 22

Shares of Loans and Other Claims on the
Nonfinancial Sector at the End of 1975

| Institution | Billions of French Francs | Percent |
|---|---|---|
| *Central Bank (4.1%)* | | |
| Banque de France | 56.6 | 4.1 |
| *Deposit-Taking Institutions (48.3%)* | | |
| National Banks | 243.4 | 17.5 |
| Other Deposit Banks | 157.6 | 11.3 |
| Investment Banks | 26.0 | 1.9 |
| Popular Banks | 34.9 | 2.5 |
| Agricultural Credit Banks | 177.5 | 12.8 |
| Mutual Credit Banks | 18.3 | 1.3 |
| Ordinary Savings Banks | 13.9 | 1.0 |
| *Long-Term Credit Institutions (32.9%)* | | |
| Long-Term Credit Banks | 8.9 | 0.6 |
| Foreign Trade Bank | 12.0 | 0.9 |
| Crédit National | 25.6 | 1.8 |
| Crédit Foncier | 52.7 | 3.8 |
| Caisse des Dépots et Consignations | 222.0 | 16.0 |
| Social Housing Loans Fund | 74.2 | 5.3 |
| Other Special Credit Institutions | 11.5 | 0.8 |
| Treasury and Fonds de Développement Economique et Social | 51.0 | 3.7 |
| *Investing Institutions (9.3%)* | | |
| Insurance Companies | 97.9 | 7.1 |
| Mutual Funds (SICAVs) | 25.0 | 1.8 |
| Common Investment Funds | 6.0 | 0.4 |
| *Other Financial Institutions (5.4%)* | | |
| Cooperative Credit Institutions | 14.4 | 1.0 |
| Finance Companies | 53.4 | 3.9 |
| Regional Development Corporations | 7.1 | 0.5 |
| | 1,389.9 | 100.0 |

Source: *Banking Systems Abroad,* Table 8, p. 129.

equities. Additional deductions are allowed for children: 500 francs for each of the first two children and 1,000 francs for each subsequent child.

By the end of 1978 an estimated one million new shareholders, half of whom were first-time equity investors, had placed about 3.5 billion francs in the stock market, and stock prices on the Paris Bourse increased about 44 percent in the same year.[6] However, if we employ

6. R. E. Wubbels, "The French Economic Miracle," *Financial Analysts Journal,* July–August 1979, p. 24.

the conventional partition of financial markets into the categories of bank credit (which consists essentially of commercial and personal loans), bonds, and equities or stocks, total bank credit remains more than twice the sum of the other two categories and is estimated to account for about 80 percent of the French money supply. During the 1970s, moreover, bonds outstanding were on the average only about 25 percent of the total of bank credit, while the value of (quoted) bonds exceeded that of (quoted) equities by 50 percent. In the latter part of the 1970s the amount of net bond financing after retirements had been about three times that of equity financing. Bond financing exceeds equity financing principally because public ownership in France is so extensive and because public enterprises are almost exclusively financed by fixed income securities (bonds issued by public enterprises, in turn, account for about 70 to 80 percent of all bonds issued during the 1970s). On the other hand, equity financing is by far the most important source of funds for private, nonfinancial firms, and this has been the case for many years.[7]

Although much of the financial sector of the French economy can be regarded from an administrative point of view as part of the government, many banks function in large measure as independents, at least in terms of their macroeconomic influence. The part of the system that is under the direct control of the government consists of the Banque de France, the Treasury, and selected other intermediaries. The Treasury loans out or allocates the funds collected by the postal checking system through such intermediaries as the Fonds de développement économique et social, the Crédit national, and the Crédit foncier (which specializes in mortgage financing), and the funds of the savings banks are for the most part allocated by the Caisse des dépôts et consignations (CDC) to various other intermediaries. However, the national agricultural bank (CNCA) and the popular banks possess large amounts of assets that can be managed independently, although they function as government organizations with respect to some classes of financial operations. Mélitz states: "It is commonly agreed therefore that as far as questions of macroeconomic analysis are concerned – issues of credit and money aggregates and interest rates – the banking sector outside the immediate control of the authorities should be seen as including the CNCA, the popular banks, the Banque française du commerce extérieur, the three nationalized banks, together with the other listed [registered] banks."[8] The governmental portion of the financial system thus can be taken as

7. Mélitz, p. 5.
8. Ibid., p. 4.

consisting of the Banque de France, the Treasury, the postal checking system, and the savings banks.

Table 23 shows a distribution of total money liabilities in France for the years selected and indicates that, however intricate the nature of government control may be, the government sector's portion of all financial liabilities has declined from about 62 percent in 1963 to about 46 percent in 1978, whereas the private sector's portion has risen from about 38 percent in 1963 to approximately 57 percent in 1978.

## The French System of Credit Allocation

There are three major interest rates in France, one in the money market (this is essentially the rediscount rate on short-term financial instruments), one on bank credit (for short- and medium-term commercial loans), and one on bonds. Money market rates are essentially fixed by the Banque de France through its rate of intervention (*taux de l'argent au jour le jour*). Actually, there is not just one intervention rate but a number of them which vary according to the risk class of securities and their maturities. The rate for Treasury bonds (*bons du Trésor*) usually differs from that for high-quality financial paper (*les effets privés de première catégorie*); the daily rate can differ from the weekly and monthly rates, and the three- and six-month rates usually differ from one another, etc. The Banque de France uses these rates as monetary policy instruments and sets them in accordance with economic policy considerations, particularly those relating to exchange rate management. The Treasury and other government agencies essentially determine the level and term structure of interest rates on bonds in order, as it is sometimes said, to promote an orderly market.[9] Relative to these two classes of rates, the bank credit rate is free in the sense that it is determined by supply and demand forces operating around a "managed float" influence which flows through the financial system from the intervention rates set by the Banque de France. One can readily understand, even from this brief discussion, why it is common for French writers on monetary matters to observe that interest rates are largely determined by "conditions of external equilibrium" (i.e., by exchange rate influences and policies).

The complex relationship between these three rates, which is unlike that in other countries, has many ramifications, among them

9. Private firms are free to arrange bond issues, but the Treasury must be informed when details with one or more banks have been arranged. The market for such bonds is small and only a few significant issues are floated each year.

## TABLE 23

### Distribution of Monetary Liabilities in France
(All figures except percents in billions of French francs)

| | | Government's Total Monetary Liabilities | | | | | Private Sector Liabilities | | | | |
|---|---|---|---|---|---|---|---|---|---|---|---|
| Year | Currency | Postal Checking Accounts | Deposits with Savings Banks | Nontransferable Treasury Bonds | Total | Percent of All Liabilities | Demand Deposits | Term Deposits | Total | Percent of All Liabilities | Total All Liabilities |
| 1963 | 57.55 | 20.06 | 43.38 | 28.90 | 149.89 | 62.03 | 72.15 | 19.60 | 91.75 | 37.97 | 241.64 |
| 1970 | 75.88 | 33.62 | 112.02 | 32.19 | 253.71 | 51.86 | 124.64 | 110.90 | 235.54 | 48.14 | 489.25 |
| 1978 | 131.94 | 82.59 | 432.92 | 46.39 | 693.84 | 43.31 | 362.02 | 545.99 | 908.01 | 56.69 | 1601.85 |

Source: Adapted from J. Mélitz, The French Financial System: Mechanisms and Propositions of Reform (Paris: Institut national de la statistique et des études économiques, 1980), Table 1, p. 3.

that the term structure of interest rates determined in the market does not adequately reflect anticipations about future interest rates. It has been emphasized that considerable shifts in the interest rate structure can take place as a result of movements between the bond market and the bank credit market without causing any changes in expectations about the spectrum of future interest rates.[10]

The relationship between the interest rate on bonds and that on bank credit is of great importance to monetary policy, and a discussion of it will also throw light on our considerations of problems of investment, economic growth, and entrepreneurship that appear in other sections. The Treasury, which determines the interest rate structure on bonds, usually follows policies which have the effect of keeping interest rates low, both in real terms and relative to what might be called a "market clearing" interest rate. The result is a "cheap credit" situation (favorable, no doubt, to the government because of the vast importance of bond financing for public enterprises); borrowers usually desire to issue more debt at this rate than lenders wish to acquire, so that it is necessary to ration the existing quantity of credit supplied to borrowers. Thus, there is "always a queue on the borrowing side of the bond market."[11] Positioned first in the queue are the Treasury, government-owned financial institutions, and the public enterprises such as Electricité de France, the postal system, the railways, and the like. Next in the queue are the nationalized firms operating in the private sector, such as Renault and Charbonnages de France, and the private financial institutions. Last in the queue are private nonfinancial firms, which therefore bear the greatest burden under this system of rationing and must either turn to internal financing – which they do extensively when profits are adequate – or to the market for bank credit (there is no commercial paper market in France).[12] This residual claimant status with respect to bond financing largely accounts for the fact that bank credit is about four times the size of bond credit in France (bank credit is so important that the French economy is sometimes referred to as a credit economy rather than a money economy).

When a private firm turns to the market for bank credit, however, it encounters yet another system of priorities, one which differs from that in the bond market. This system defines a "privileged circuit" in which some firms can obtain financing with terms and rates that are

10. Mélitz, p. 13; see also C. de Boissieu, *La Structure des taux d'intérêt* (Paris: Economica, 1976).
11. Mélitz, p. 8. The length of the queue may be reduced somewhat by substituting equity financing for bonds, but these instruments are poor substitutes for one another.
12. Ibid., p. 9.

more favorable than those available to others. Outside this circuit the price of credit is determined by supply and demand forces. The circuit operates through loans distributed by various financial intermediaries under the Treasury, through preferential refinancing terms on selected loans to commercial banks and on selected mortgages, and through exemptions to the *encadrements du crédit*, or credit growth ceilings.

## The Encadrements du Crédit

Because bank credit to firms and individuals is the largest source of money creation in France, the regulation of bank credit is the principal tool of monetary policy. The overall level of bank credit is controlled with considerable effectiveness—if not efficiency—through the *encadrements du crédit*. These credit growth ceilings were first instituted in the 1960s as a corrective for what was believed to be overlending by some banks. Originally intended to be used sparingly and temporarily, they were reimposed in late 1972 and since 1974 have become a major instrument of quantitative credit control. Under the *encadrements*, each bank is assigned a specified ceiling on credit growth to which it must adhere during a specified, ensuing time period (usually six months). If a bank lends in excess of its assigned ceiling, it must deposit additional non-interest-bearing reserves in the Banque de France. The amount of this deposit is calculated according to the formula

$$T = (0.30 + 0.15X)X,$$

where $X$ is the number of percentage points of credit extended in excess of the ceiling and $T$ is the ratio of the additional required reserves to the credit extended in excess of the ceiling. Thus, if a bank lends an amount equal to one percentage point in excess of its ceiling, then $T = (0.30 + 0.15[1])1 = .45$; this means that 45 percent of the excess amount must be placed with the Banque de France in the form of a non-interest-bearing deposit. As another example, if a bank exceeds its ceiling by 1.5 percentage points, the equation gives $T = .7875$, or 78.75 percent.

The impact of the *encadrements* on residual claimant borrowers in the private sector is clearly very considerable; if a bank is to transgress its credit growth ceilings profitably, it must charge extremely high interest rates to these additional borrowers. Thus, it is not surprising that the condition of exceeding the *encadrements* was initially referred to as "super hell."

The government, in formulating and applying monetary policies, attempts to establish a maximum level of increase in credit for a given year, which is translated through a complex administrative process into *encadrements* for each bank. It must be stressed that the monetary authorities in France cannot effectively control monetary expansion either by controlling bank liquidity or by administering interest rates. The former is unsatisfactory because commercial banks depend almost entirely on the Banque de France to meet their reserve requirements, and the Banque must in essence provide commercial banks with sufficient reserves to meet their liquidity needs in order to prevent the generation of undesirable pressures on money market rates. This means that the Banque de France finds it extremely difficult to control the quantity of reserve money in circulation (the monetary base). Controlling the money supply by close supervision of interest rates is also impossible because of constraints relating to exchange rate policy, the pursuit of policies to encourage domestic investment, as well as a variety of other reasons. Thus, the authorities are largely confined to controlling money supply growth "at the retail level" by controlling bank credit via the *encadrements*.[13] This results in a full-fledged *dirigiste* system of credit control, through which the authorities have considerable influence on bank operations, on the total volume of credit, and hence on the money supply.

Quite apart from its *dirigiste* character, the system of *encadrements*, as currently applied, has a number of important defects. Until 1978 almost all government-subsidized credit relating to exports, agriculture, housing, investment in energy-saving activities, and a variety of other uses was exempted from the credit growth ceilings. Not surprisingly, credit flows into these exempted investment outlets grew much more rapidly than those into activities subject to the ceilings. Because of this "overflow," whose size was impossible to predict and impossible to manage in a macroeconomic sense, the *encadrements* did not produce the monetary policy effects that were intended. The government attempted to ameliorate this problem in 1978 by restricting the exemptions to some extent, but because the exemptions have important political implications, the restrictions were moderate and reduced the volume of lending for exempted activities by only about 25 percent.[14] Even after the restrictions were imposed, disproportion in credit flows persisted: in 1979 the average annual rate of increase in bank credit subject to *encadrements* was about 9 percent, as contrasted with about 27 percent for exempted bank credit. Most of the latter was attributed to financing in the property markets, where

13. Organization for Economic Cooperation and Development, *Monetary Policy in France* (Paris: OECD, 1974), chap. 3.
14. Mélitz, p. 17.

demand also happened to receive an additional stimulus from the removal of consumer credit (installment purchase) restrictions.[15]

There are many other shortcomings to the *encadrements* system. The establishing of credit growth ceilings for all commercial banks tends to maintain the existing size distribution of banks, thereby tending to reduce competition between banks. It is relatively difficult for small banks to grow (but exceptions can be found: Banque Hervet began as a small provincial bank, opened branches in Paris, concentrated in loans to medium-sized firms, and is now a profitable and growing enterprise with an association with the Harris Bank of Chicago). Also, to the extent that bank credit is more difficult to obtain for firms outside the privileged circuit, as has been noted, the *encadrements* serve to exert considerable upward pressures on interest rates for such firms. On the other hand, by making bond financing and loans available at lower rates to government agencies or to firms operating in activities that the government seeks to encourage, some important social costs of government subsidies are concealed from the public view. As we have seen, the system also encourages internal rather than external financing, so that internal financing ratios for French firms are less favorable than for comparable firms in other Western countries.

The *encadrements* (and other features of the financial markets) have contributed to the persistent shortage of long-term capital in the private sector in France. Private corporations are encouraged, in effect, to hold financial instruments of shorter maturities than they would prefer or than might be optimal in a resource allocation sense. The shift in the term structure of investments towards shorter maturities has been a matter of growing concern to French monetary economists. Net new long- and medium-term debt for French businesses was about 12 percent lower in 1979 than in 1973, for example, whereas net new short-term bank financing increased by 118 percent over the same period. Another closely related problem, often the subject of complaints by French businessmen, is that of supplier credits.[16] These are short-term credits extended to firms by others which supply goods and services to them; they account for as much as half the short-term debt of many companies and represent an important way for business firms to evade the *encadrements*. Moreover, difficulties associated with supplier credits have exacerbated management problems, particularly in small and medium-sized firms and even in some large firms having extensive international operations.

15. Organization for Economic Cooperation and Development, *France* (Paris: OECD, May 1980), pp. 36–39.
16. *France in Transition* (Geneva: Business International Corporation, 1979), pp. 102–3.

The various credit restrictions, including the *encadrements*, together with the heavy reliance on bank credit, have led many private firms to utilize a consortium, or pool of banks, in order to attract funds, with negotiations taking place through the chief banker or consortium leader (*chef de file*). These negotiations often lead to a ritualized arrangement in which every change in a firm's use of bank credit is allocated to the banks composing the pool according to precisely defined percentages for each member. Such negotiations also aggravate management problems of firms and produce cumbersome procedures for all concerned.

Much analysis has been given to the detrimental influences of the *encadrements* and other rigidities of the French financial system, but even the brief treatment given here suggests that these influences exert considerable downward pressures on the volume of investment in France, as well as on the rate of economic growth and the volume of employment. They also exert unfavorable influences on corporate risk taking in both direct and indirect (often subtle) ways, and are probably important causes of the relative stagnation of investment that has taken place in France since 1973.

## Monetary Policies, 1975–81

Money supply growth is an appropriate starting point for a consideration of monetary policy. Table 24 shows Gross Domestic Product, M2 (*masse monétaire*), M3 (*ensemble des liquidités*), and various growth rates. The latter are percent changes in the corresponding variable for the four-quarter period terminating in the given quarter, so that 17.24 percent, the first entry in the percent change column for M2, is the growth rate or percent change in M2 from 1970.1 through 1971.1.[17]

Growth rates in M2 were high from 1971.1 through 1976.3, the quarter when the Barre program began to be implemented. These growth rates exceeded growth rates in nominal GDP in all but 3 of the four-quarter periods from 1970.1 through 1976.3. Another way of making this point is to note that in the 23 four-quarter periods used in this discussion, M2 growth exceeded GDP growth in 20 cases, or in about 87 percent of these four-quarter periods. Alternatively, over the span of 18 four-quarter periods in the interval from 1976.4 through 1981.1, M2 growth exceeded GDP growth in 6 quarters, or in 33.3

---

17. As indicated in Chapter 1, M2 includes coins and currency outside the Banque de France; current accounts at the Banque de France, Treasury, and post office; time, demand, and savings deposits; certificates of deposit; and time deposits at the Treasury (M2 is similar to M1-B in the United States). M3 consists of M2 plus various liquid liabilities of the Treasury, post office, and other government agencies.

TABLE 24

Quarterly Nominal GDP, M2, M3, and
Four-Quarter Growth Rates, 1971–81
(All data except percents in billions of francs,
seasonally adjusted)

| Quarter | Gross Domestic Product | Percent Change in GDP | Masse Monétaire (M2) | Percent Change in M2 | Ensemble des Liquidités (M3) | Percent Change in M3 |
|---|---|---|---|---|---|---|
| 1971.1 | 209.3 | 11.63 | 362.29 | 17.24 | 512.00 | 15.81 |
| .2 | 214.6 | 10.73 | 377.81 | 19.13 | 533.59 | 17.88 |
| .3 | 220.5 | 11.53 | 391.25 | 19.19 | 551.90 | 17.80 |
| .4 | 228.0 | 11.98 | 406.47 | 17.63 | 571.98 | 16.68 |
| 1972.1 | 234.8 | 12.18 | 426.20 | 17.64 | 596.78 | 16.56 |
| .2 | 241.1 | 12.35 | 450.88 | 19.34 | 626.44 | 17.40 |
| .3 | 249.1 | 12.97 | 470.00 | 20.13 | 650.88 | 17.93 |
| .4 | 256.1 | 12.32 | 481.64 | 18.49 | 668.38 | 16.85 |
| 1973.1 | 264.9 | 12.82 | 489.02 | 14.74 | 681.86 | 14.26 |
| .2 | 272.7 | 13.11 | 513.01 | 13.78 | 711.31 | 13.55 |
| .3 | 281.0 | 12.67 | 531.30 | 13.04 | 735.64 | 13.02 |
| .4 | 295.6 | 15.42 | 553.19 | 14.86 | 762.94 | 14.15 |
| 1974.1 | 304.3 | 14.87 | 574.11 | 17.40 | 790.57 | 15.94 |
| .2 | 315.9 | 15.84 | 591.02 | 15.21 | 813.79 | 14.41 |
| .3 | 327.5 | 16.55 | 612.58 | 15.30 | 843.87 | 14.71 |
| .4 | 330.7 | 11.87 | 640.93 | 15.86 | 878.86 | 15.19 |
| 1975.1 | 343.7 | 12.95 | 662.62 | 15.42 | 911.38 | 15.28 |
| .2 | 357.2 | 13.07 | 687.49 | 16.32 | 948.46 | 16.55 |
| .3 | 368.7 | 12.58 | 720.84 | 17.67 | 995.29 | 17.94 |
| .4 | 382.7 | 15.72 | 757.21 | 18.14 | 1048.15 | 19.26 |
| 1976.1 | 397.1 | 15.71 | 786.23 | 18.65 | 1092.87 | 19.91 |
| .2 | 414.6 | 15.87 | 817.69 | 18.94 | 1138.08 | 19.99 |
| .3 | 426.4 | 15.62 | 836.20 | 16.00 | 1171.49 | 17.70 |
| .4 | 439.9 | 14.95 | 854.18 | 12.81 | 1201.25 | 14.61 |
| 1977.1 | 453.9 | 14.06 | 883.85 | 12.42 | 1243.84 | 13.81 |
| .2 | 463.7 | 11.67 | 903.97 | 10.55 | 1276.95 | 12.20 |
| .3 | 476.8 | 11.73 | 944.01 | 12.89 | 1330.07 | 13.54 |
| .4 | 490.3 | 11.03 | 973.04 | 13.92 | 1376.08 | 14.55 |
| 1978.1 | 504.1 | 10.82 | 1000.28 | 13.17 | 1419.52 | 14.12 |
| .2 | 528.0 | 13.63 | 1032.67 | 14.24 | 1467.29 | 14.91 |
| .3 | 544.0 | 13.90 | 1067.38 | 13.07 | 1520.14 | 14.29 |
| .4 | 563.4 | 15.27 | 1090.68 | 12.09 | 1559.86 | 13.36 |
| 1979.1 | 579.2 | 15.22 | 1140.05 | 13.97 | 1631.68 | 14.95 |
| .2 | 597.0 | 13.67 | 1173.31 | 13.62 | 1681.50 | 14.60 |
| .3 | 621.8 | 14.62 | 1205.99 | 12.99 | 1729.83 | 13.79 |
| .4 | 641.4 | 13.93 | 1247.48 | 14.38 | 1784.89 | 14.43 |
| 1980.1 | 661.1 | 14.14 | 1284.46 | 12.67 | 1835.58 | 12.50 |
| .2 | 678.3 | 13.62 | 1307.62 | 11.45 | 1872.64 | 11.37 |

TABLE 24 (continued)

| Quarter | Gross Domestic Product | Percent Change in GDP | Masse Monétaire (M2) | Percent Change in M2 | Ensemble des Liquidités (M3) | Percent Change in M3 |
|---|---|---|---|---|---|---|
| .3 | 703.7 | 13.17 | 1339.10 | 11.04 | 1922.11 | 11.12 |
| .4 | 712.4 | 11.07 | 1369.06 | 9.75 | 1970.52 | 10.40 |
| 1981.1 | 721.6 | 9.15 | 1422.27 | 10.73 | 2043.99 | 11.35 |
| .2 | * | * | 1477.70 | 13.01 | 2114.00 | 12.89 |

Sources: For GDP, 1971.1 through 1975.4, Organization for Economic Cooperation and Development, Quarterly National Accounts Bulletin, 1966–80, IV (Paris: OECD, 1980), p. 76. For GDP, 1976.1 through 1981.1, OECD, Quarterly National Accounts Bulletin II (Paris: OECD, 1981), p. 55.
Notes: Percent changes are for the four-quarter period terminating in the given quarter. M2 and M3 data were supplied to the author by the Institut national de la statistique et des études économiques.
Quarterly data for M2 and M3 are monthly values for the final month of the quarter.
*Not available.

percent of these cases. On the basis of these measures it can be said  that there was a substantial reduction in money supply growth relative to GDP growth in the latter period as compared to the pre-1976.4 period, although money supply growth was larger than some had hoped it would be.

Figure 4 shows a plot of the growth rates in nominal GDP and M2 from 1971.1 through 1981.1. The correspondence between these two time series beginning in 1976.4 was clearly much closer than in the earlier period, and both time series experienced fluctuations of smaller amplitudes than formerly. Figure 5 plots the growth rates in nominal GDP and in M3 during the same set of years; similar behavior before and after 1976.4 can be observed, although M3 displays somewhat more volatility than M2 and also tends to have somewhat higher growth rates after 1976 than M2. Figure 6 shows a plot of M2 and M3 growth rates.

There was also a major shift in the announced monetary policy during the Barre years. For the first time in French economic history, a target for total money supply growth was announced by the government (during previous years the only announced objective was related to the growth of part of the domestic credit from the banks). M2 was targeted to grow at a rate of 12.5 percent for the year 1977 (December to December), an objective closely related to the forecasted annual growth rate in nominal GDP of 12.5 percent for the year. Growth in controlled bank credit (i.e., bank credit subject to the encadrements) was set for 8 percent for the year. These targets were

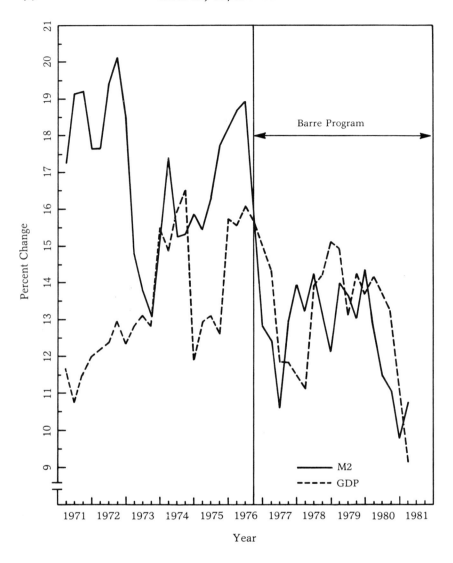

Figure 4.    Four-Quarter Percent Changes in M2 and in GDP, 1971–81

based on an assumption that foreign exchange reserves (referred to as the "external sector") and the Treasury would, on balance, have a neutral influence on money creation during the year.

The policy of announcing money supply growth targets was continued at the end of 1977. A growth target of 12 percent for M2 during 1978 was announced and growth in controlled bank credit was again

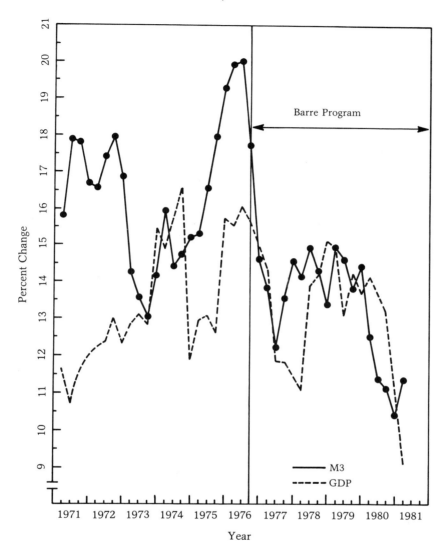

**Figure 5.    Four-Quarter Percent Changes in M3 and in GDP, 1971–81**

set for 8 percent. An annual percent growth of 12.5 percent for nominal GDP was forecast for 1978, and the money supply growth target
was set slightly below this forecasted value. As was the case for the
1977 targets for M2 and controlled bank credit, the 1978 targets
assumed that the external sector and the Treasury would be neutral
with respect to money creation during the year.

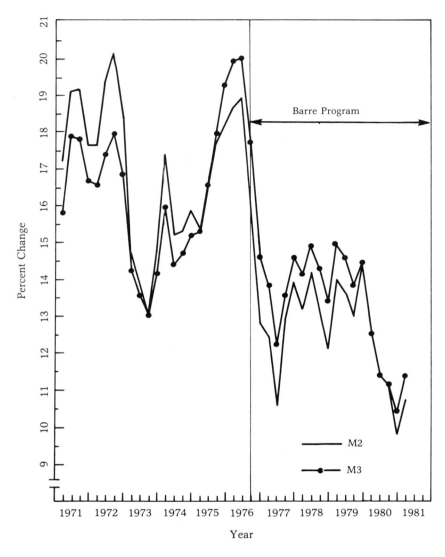

**Figure 6.    Four-Quarter Percent Changes in M2 and M3, 1971–81**

    In 1979, an M2 target was set at 11 percent, which was two percentage points below the forecast of 13 percent for nominal GDP growth for the year and one percentage point below the M2 target of the previous year. Controlled bank credit was also tightened, being set about one percentage point below that for 1978. The monetary authorities set these targets for 1979 on the assumption of a net increase in the money supply of about 20 billion francs flowing from foreign ex-  change reserve movements and money creation on the part of the Treasury. This alteration was deemed necessary because the assumption of neutrality of new money influence from these two sources had not been satisfied in 1978, nor had it been satisfied with respect to the external sector in 1977. In 1980 the M2 target was again set at 11 percent.

The question naturally arises as to the extent of the effect of these monetary targets on inflation in France and on money supply growth. It is perhaps impossible to determine whether the targets, per se, played a role in the reduction in the money supply growth rates noted above. Whether the targets had a favorable influence on inflation expectations in France is also difficult to determine; but a critical issue with respect to expected inflation is not so much the existence of targets, but whether the targeted levels were maintained or exceeded. This question can be examined and Table 25 summarizes the situation. The monetary target was exceeded in 1977, 1978, and 1979, but not in 1980. According to Table 24, the growth in M2 for 1978 (December to December) was 12.09 percent. The interval of 14 to 15 percent, the estimate developed by Fourçans (see note at bottom of Table 25), is chosen as more informative because it corrects for the effect (asserted by Fourçans) of a short-run arrangement made in

TABLE 25

Actual Yearly Growth of M2 and Targeted Growth,
1975–1980

| Year | Targeted Growth in M2 (Percent) | Actual Yearly Growth in M2 (Percent Change from December to December) | Target Exceeded? | Percent Change in CPI, December to December |
|---|---|---|---|---|
| 1975 | None | 18.7 | – | 9.94 |
| 1976 | None | 12.86 | – | 10.01 |
| 1977 | 12.5 | 13.78 | Yes | 9.19 |
| 1978 | 12 | 14–15[a] | Yes | 9.45 |
| 1979 | 11 | 14.43 | Yes | 11.54 |
| 1980 | 11 | 9.75 | No | 13.59 |

Sources: Table 23; for CPI, calculations made from CPI data in Organization for Economic Cooperation and Development, Main Economic Indicators, Historical Statistics, 1960–1979 (Paris: OECD, 1980), p. 296; 1980 data supplied by OECD.

Notes: M2 data are seasonally adjusted. Percent changes in CPI are calculated from data that are not seasonally adjusted.

[a] Estimate given in A. Fourçans, "Has Monsieur Barre's Experiment in Monetarism Failed?," the Paris Lecture given at the City University of London, May 13, 1980, p. 18.

December 1978 between the Treasury and the Banque de France which "sterilized" 27.5 billion francs for a period of about three weeks.

In order to examine monetary policy in greater detail, it is helpful to distinguish subperiods in the interval since 1976. The subperiod extending from 1976.2 to 1977.2 can be regarded as one in which a tight monetary policy was pursued. The growth rate in M2 dropped from 18.94 percent to 10.55 percent, and interest rates rose from about 7 to 10 percent. These were major changes over the previous several years (during the same period inflation rose by 10.23 percent, as measured by the change in the CPI). From 1977.3 through the end of 1978 monetary policy was considerably looser; money supply growth exceeded targeted levels and interest rates declined to nearly 6.5 percent by the end of 1978, while inflation rose to just under 10 percent. Furthermore, neither foreign exchange inflows nor the Treasury was a neutral influence on money supply growth during this period (which had been assumed, as noted earlier, in the setting of monetary targets). There was substantial money creation from the Treasury because of an increase in the government deficit which was financed in large measure by means of Treasury bills placed with the banks.[18]

The year 1979 provided even more complex challenges for economic policy. The domestic economy was buoyant, and attempts were made to tighten money policy. M2 growth was assigned a target of 11 percent, which, as we have noted, was lower than that for 1978 and lower than the growth in GDP forecast for 1979; and the credit growth norms were stiffened. There was, however, a large increase in credit to households, some of which was in the form of credit exempted from the *encadrements*, and, overall, bank credit (both controlled and restricted credit) grew relatively rapidly, as we have seen. Interest rates rose sharply in the second half of the year, after falling throughout most of the first half; the long-term rate on top-quality private securities approached 12.5 percent and short-term rates exceeded 14 percent by year-end. At the same time, the budget deficit was increasing, fueled by increases in social security and defense expenditures; about one-third of the deficit was funded by means of monetary expansion.[19] Despite the attempts at tightening, however, the money supply growth rate for the year (14.43 percent) considerably overshot the target, and inflation rose to 11.54 percent, in contrast to the previous year's increase of 9.45 percent.

It appears that a tight monetary policy was continued in 1980. The

18. OECD, *France*, May 1980, p. 37.
19. Ibid., p. 43.

growth in M2 from 1979.4 through 1980.4 was 9.75 percent (see Table 24), which was less than in any four-quarter period during the 1975–79 interval and considerably less than the growth in the money supply during the latter part of 1979. This attempt at controlling the money supply can be regarded as courageous when one recalls that a presidential election was in the offing for 1981. However, it was also true that Barre's budget for 1980 had a planned or forecasted deficit of 31 billion francs, more than twice the level of the planned deficit for 1979, and the actual deficit for 1980 was widely expected to be in excess of 50 billion francs (this budget situation was described by a French magazine as a *"frisson Keynésien"*).[20] There was also a second energy price shock, which had troubling influences beginning in late 1979: during the period 1979.4 through 1980.4, the CPI rose by 13.59 percent. Table 24 also indicates that the M2 growth rate for the four-quarter period ending in March 1981 was up by one percentage point over that for the previous quarter, and for the four-quarter period ending in June 1981 (by which time the Socialist government was in office) it had risen yet again, this time by more than two percentage points.

To summarize, monetary policy followed a tight-loose-tight sequence from 1976 through the end of 1980. Although money supply growth rates were lower than during the years prior to 1976, they exceeded (in terms of averages for the year) the targets and inflation rates, particularly for 1979 and 1980, and moved well beyond the 10 percent level. This suggests that it is unlikely that the monetary authorities were able to make much progress in reducing inflation expectations or inflation-related uncertainties, and it also appears that monetary policy was not able to contribute as much to the stabilization of the French economy as Barre's initial statement of goals had intended, nor as much as the pursuit of the goals required. Furthermore, the 1979 and 1980 inflation rates were high relative to the best years of the Barre program, and the inflation containment goals that had been stated in 1976 also went unrealized.

## Fiscal Policies, 1975–81

Measures of French budget deficits, compiled from various sources, are given in Table 26.[21] Roughly speaking, these data show that the

20. *L'Expansion,* September 7–20, 1979, pp. 28–29; cited in D. Green, "The Budget and the Plan," in *French Politics and Public Policy,* ed. P. G. Cerny and M. A. Shain (New York: St. Martin's Press, 1980), p. 114.
21. It is difficult to obtain reliable data on French budget deficits, and data are often made available only after delays extending up to two years beyond the year to which they refer. The government releases various "balance" figures which are sometimes

TABLE 26

French Budget Deficits, 1975–80
(Billions of francs)

| Year | Actual Deficit | Percent Change in Actual Deficit, Year to Year | Annual GDP | Actual Deficit as a Percent of GDP (Rounded) | Effective Budget Deficit | Effective Deficit as a Percent of GDP (Rounded) | Forecasted or Planned Deficit |
|------|------|------|------|------|------|------|------|
| 1975 | 38.011 | · · · | 1452.3 | 2.6% | 43.0 | 3.0% | · · · |
| 1976 | 20.046 | −47.3 | 1678.0 | 1.2 | 18.0 | 1.1 | · · · |
| 1977 | 18.041 | −10.0 | 1880.5 | 1.0 | 20.0 | 1.1 | · · · |
| 1978 | 34.124 | +89.1 | 2133.5 | 1.6 | 45.0 | 2.1 | 8.9 |
| 1979 | 42.000* | +23.1 | 2430.7 | 1.7 | 45.0 | 1.9 | 15.0 |
| 1980 | 51.000* | +21.4 | 2755.5 | 1.9 | · · · | · · · | 31.0 |

*Sources:* Actual deficit figures, except those denoted by an asterisk, are from D. Green, "The Budget and the Plan," in *French Politics and Public Policy,* ed. P. G. Cerny and M. A. Shain (New York: St. Martin's Press, 1980), p. 114. Annual GDP figures are from OECD data. Effective budget deficit figures are estimates prepared by Fourçans, p. 18. Fourçans's estimate for 1978 includes expenses incurred in 1978 but reported, on an accounting basis, in 1979. Estimates denoted by an asterisk were prepared by the author.

budget deficit was reduced by almost half in 1976 and again in 1977 (the first Barre budget year), as compared with that for the troubled year of 1975. The deficit rose sharply in 1978, however, almost reaching the 1975 level in nominal terms, and it continued to rise, again in nominal terms, in 1979 and 1980. Table 26 also shows the actual and "effective" deficits expressed as a percent of GDP. Since 1977, both of these deficits, as well as their corresponding percentages of GDP, have been rising, but neither has reached its 1975 level. In comparative terms, moreover, deficits as a percent of GDP, as French politicians often point out, were smaller than for some of the other Western nations (including West Germany and Great Britain in 1978 and the United States in 1980).

With respect to the allocation of resources and problems of inflation, however, the critical question is not whether France had deficits that were small in terms of GDP or small as compared with those of other Western nations, but how the deficits were financed (France has experienced high inflation rates at various times in the past when its budget deficit was no more than 1 percent of GDP). Another key question is whether there is a trend or some consistency in the growth of deficits over several years which could have had adverse influences on inflation expectations. Recent research has stressed that the relationship between contemporaneous deficits and inflation rates in the short run—if it exists at all—is not simple (both fiscal and monetary policies operate with lags). Governments have incurred rising budget deficits when inflation rates were declining (as in the United States in late 1981) and have had budget surpluses when rates of inflation were rising. Deficits which persist over several years are, of course, another matter entirely.[22]

As is well known, a government has several ways of financing defi-

taken as measures of the overall budget deficit but are usually smaller. One of these is the "balance of operations of a definitive character," which, as one might expect, excludes the "balance of operations of a temporary character" (it is very difficult to obtain a precise definition of these two terms). There are also budget accounts on "a management basis" and budget accounts on "an accounting period basis"; these reflect different ways of dealing with the timing aspects of government revenue and expenditure transactions. For several years the government has also made available, as part of its fiscal policy procedures and budgeting operations, a forecasted or planned deficit figure which has underestimated the actual deficit, as is the case in other countries as well.

22. For a careful examination of these issues see M. J. Hamburger and B. Zwick, "Deficits, Money, and Inflation," *Journal of Monetary Economics* 7 (1981):141–50; R. J. Barro, "Unanticipated Money, Output, and the Price Level in the United States," *Journal of Political Economy* 86 (1978):549–80; W. A. Niskanen, "Deficits, Government Spending and Inflation: What Is the Evidence?," *Journal of Monetary Economics* 4 (1978):591–602; and B. M. Friedman, "Crowding Out or Crowding In? Economic Consequences of Financing Budget Deficits," *Brookings Papers on Economic Activity* 3 (1978):593–655.

cits. It can create money for this purpose or it can issue bonds, or it can employ a mixture of these two approaches.[23] When a government issues bonds and the deficit is financed out of private savings, the result is less inflationary than when money creation devices (which include the sale of bonds to the central bank) are employed. In 1975 and 1976 the deficit was funded largely through money creation measures, but in 1977 the deficit was financed chiefly out of private savings resources.[24] In 1978, however, the deficit—which had almost doubled over its 1977 level—was substantially funded through money creation, and in 1979 about the same proportion of the deficit was paid for by money creation as in 1978.[25] The proportion of the 1980 deficit that was financed by money creation is unknown at this writing, but it is likely that it will turn out to be similar to that for 1978 and 1979.

With continued pressures arising from money creation since 1978, with budget deficits rising each year since 1977 (which probably caused inflation expectations to worsen), and with the inflationary pressures exerted by the second oil shock of 1979 and 1980, it is not surprising that inflation rose significantly in the second half of 1980 and early 1981. It is also reasonable to conclude that the Barre fiscal policies have had, on balance, a more inflationary impact on the economy than was consistent with his stated goals.

Why did these fiscal policies depart from the desired goals to such an extent? One can only speculate on answers to this question. One likely cause was apprehensions relating to the growth of unemployment; these contributed to stimulative budgets in several ways and, as was noted in Chapter 2, government expenditures to stimulate employment were considerable. Another contributing factor, which turned out to be extremely difficult to moderate, was the growth rate in total government spending; this rose at an annual rate of about 5 percent per year from 1970 to 1980, as compared to an annual growth of about 3 percent in real GDP over the same period. Redistributional expenditures, chiefly social benefits of various kinds, have also continued to rise; by 1979 these accounted for about 60 percent of total government expenditures and about 25 percent of GDP, in con-

23. Discussions of methods of financing deficits, the distinctions between the government's borrowing from the public and borrowing from the central bank in order to finance deficits (the latter leading to creation of what is known as "high-powered money" in the United States), are given in standard texts on macroeconomics. An example is R. Dornbusch and S. Fischer, *Macroeconomics* (New York: McGraw-Hill, 1978), chap. 14, "The Budget, Government Financing, and the Public Debt."

24. OECD, *France,* May 1980, p. 37.

25. A Fourçans, "Has Monsieur Barre's Experiment in Monetarism Failed?," the Paris Lecture given at the City University of London, May 13, 1980, p. 13.

trast to about 25 percent and 17 percent, respectively, in 1973.[26] Moreover, the French social security system has had a deficit every year since 1974 (with the exception of 1980); by 1980 it was estimated that persons who are economically active, about 40 percent of the population, contribute to the support of the remaining 60 percent who are inactive.[27] Facing these constraints is a chilling prospect for any economic policymaker, particularly when an election is not far off.

## Stabilizing the Franc and Balance of Payment Policies, 1975-81

The strong balance of payments performance of the French economy was one of the more important successes of the Barre program. From a current account deficit of nearly US$ 6 billion in 1976, France moved to a deficit of about half this amount in 1977, and by the end of 1978 to a surplus of US$ 3.8 billion. This was a remarkable performance, particularly the turnaround from deficit to surplus – equivalent to US$ 6.8 billion – during the period 1977 to 1978 (see Table 27). Moreover, export volume grew by more than 6 percent in each of these two years and by 10 percent in 1979, so French producers were also making progress in increasing their share of world markets.

The second oil crisis, in the course of which the nominal dollar price of oil more than doubled between the end of 1978 and early 1980, generated great pressures on the domestic economy, vastly complicating the government's foreign exchange stabilization program. By the end of 1979, France's surplus on current account had dropped to US$ 1.5 billion but did not go into deficit, largely because the oil price rises in that year were offset by the surge in demand for France's exports and by a strong increase in the invisibles account (tourist expenditures; fees for financial and legal services, and insurance; interest and dividends; port and freight charges; etc.). In 1980, however, these offsetting factors were of much smaller magnitudes, and the current account registered a deficit of US$ 7.8 billion.

Table 27 indicates that other countries, notably West Germany and Japan, also experienced sharp deteriorations in their current accounts in 1979 and 1980. West Germany had its first deficits in more than 20 years and experienced a whopping decline of US$ 21.3 billion over this two-year period (current account deficits were continuing as recently as mid-1981). West Germany had the largest current account

26. OECD, *France,* May 1980, p, 45.
27. "France Enacts Measures to Rein in a Runaway Social Security System," *International Herald Tribune,* December 3, 1981, p. 3.

TABLE 27

Current Account Balances in
France and Selected Other Countries, 1970–80
(In $US billions)

| Year | France | United States | West Germany | Italy | Nether-lands | U.K. | Japan | Canada |
|------|--------|---------------|--------------|-------|--------------|------|-------|--------|
| 1970 | 0.1 | 2.3 | 0.9 | 0.9 | -0.5 | 1.9 | 2.0 | 1.1 |
| 1975 | 0.0 | 18.3 | 4.0 | -0.6 | 2.0 | -3.7 | -0.7 | -4.7 |
| 1976 | -5.9 | 4.4 | 3.9 | -2.9 | 2.7 | -2.0 | 3.7 | -3.9 |
| 1977 | -3.0 | -14.1 | 4.1 | 2.3 | 0.3 | -0.5 | 10.9 | -4.0 |
| 1978 | 3.8 | -14.1 | 9.2 | 6.2 | -1.4 | 1.2 | 16.5 | -4.4 |
| 1979 | 1.5 | 1.4 | -5.3 | 5.1 | -2.3 | -3.5 | -8.8 | -4.4 |
| 1980 | -7.8 | 3.7 | -16.0 | -10.0 | -2.8 | 5.3 | -10.7 | -1.3 |

*Source: International Economic Indicators* (Washington, D.C.: U.S. Department of Commerce, September 1981), p. 53.

deficit of any major industrial nation in 1980. This was brought about by a combination of escalating oil prices, a relatively stimulative fiscal policy, and large tourist expenditures by Germans abroad. France's domestic energy price response was better in this period than in the period following the first oil shock; the government took steps to raise energy prices relatively quickly, and monetary policy was in a tight phase at this time. One result was that the 1980 current account deficit turned out to be less than West Germany's.

Exchange rate developments were also generally favorable from the end of 1976 until about the third quarter of 1980. Figure 7 shows one measure of exchange rate performance, the MERM measure of effective exchange rates determined by the International Monetary Fund (IMF). This is an index (1975 = 100) which combines the exchange rates between the franc and 17 other major currencies. The weights in this index are derived from the IMF's multilateral exchange rate model (hence the acronym MERM) and are calculated from a base of exchange rates for the year 1977. The weights employed take into account (through the MERM model) the size of trade flows among the countries whose currencies are involved, as well as relevant price elasticities and feedback effects of exchange rate changes on domestic prices and costs. From early 1977 through the first quarter of 1980 the franc fluctuated around a rising trend against the 17 major currencies in the MERM measure. This was a favorable development for French consumers and wealth holders; but, of course, it had other economic implications as well.

Figure 8 displays quarterly averages of the exchange rate of the franc against the U.S. dollar. The number of francs required to pur-

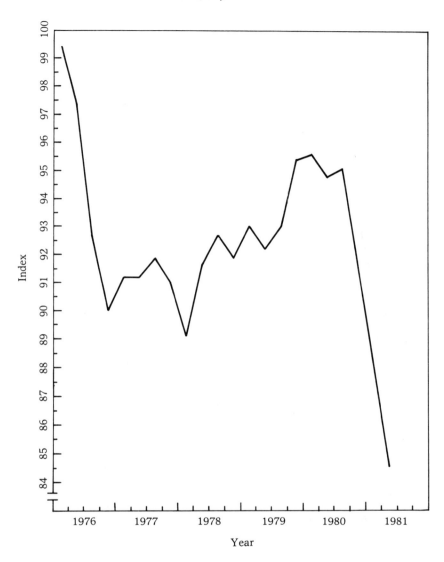

**Figure 7.    Effective Exchange Rates (MERM), Quarterly, 1976–81**

chase a dollar fluctuated around a markedly downward trend until the third quarter of 1980.[28] This had beneficial effects in France, notably on her energy import bill, because most of the energy imports

28. After September 1980 the number of francs per dollar (monthly averages) began rising and continued to rise through July 1981. Although there was some softening in August, it remained high until late in 1981, when this discussion was written.

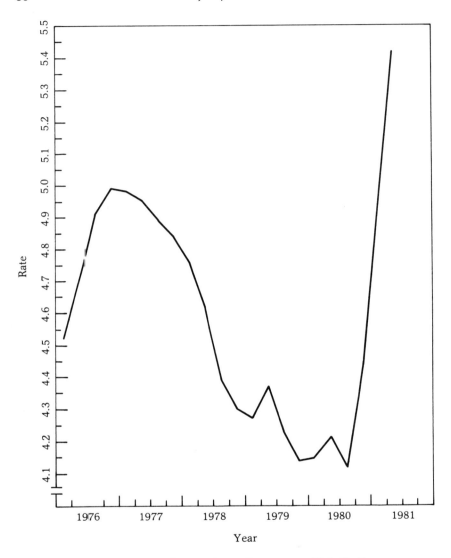

**Figure 8.    Exchange Rate, Francs per U.S. Dollar,
Quarterly Averages, 1976–81**

are denominated in U.S. dollars.[29] Figure 9 shows a plot of index numbers (end of 1972 = 100) of the value of the deutsche mark against the French franc from 1976 through the third quarter of 1981. This has displayed a reasonably stable pattern since about mid-1977.

29. Assessments of the impact of exchange rate movements are complex, as is pointed out in introductory courses in international economics, and a wide collection of interactions is possible before new equilibrium positions are approached. For example, if the

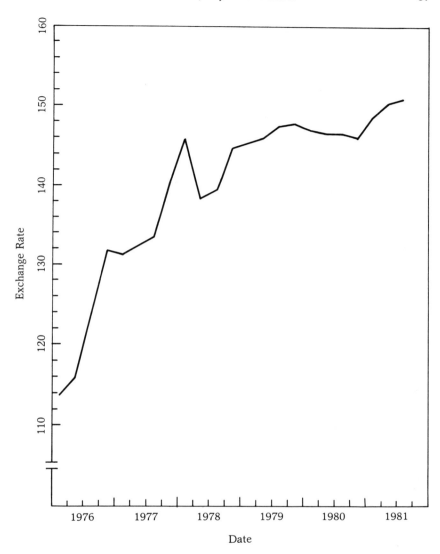

**Figure 9. Values of the Deutsche Mark against the French Franc, Final Month of Quarter, 1976–81**

franc rises against the U.S. dollar, a franc then exchanges for more U.S. currency than previously, U.S. goods are cheaper for persons holding francs, and there is an upward influence on the demand for U.S. goods and on imports into France from the U.S. Simultaneously, French goods for a U.S. consumer become more costly, there is a downward influence on demand for French goods and on exports to the U.S. from France, in turn reverberating on the domestic economy in France, and so on. In time, such movements have an impact on France's balance of payments, etc. This discussion ignores the influences of a rising franc against the dollar vis-à-vis France's energy imports which are, as noted above, denominated in dollars.

It should be mentioned that economic policies of the Barre period in effect forced domestic producers to face increasing competition in international markets, which they did reasonably well. The improvement in the manufactures trade balance for 1977, which followed the large gain resulting from the franc devaluation in 1976, was followed in turn by similar improvements in 1978 and 1979.

The foreign exchange and gold reserve situation for France was also favorable during the period 1975–80 (see Table 28). This may have reflected increasing confidence in the franc as well as improved perceptions of the soundness of underlying economic developments in France. In any case, the French reserve situation continued to improve in 1980 even after the current account balance began to worsen.

The Barre balance of payments policies were built around three principal features: avoiding the depreciation of the franc as a method of adjustment, promoting French exports, and expanding the financing of France's trade deficit abroad. We have already noted the success of the first of these. Export promotion was encouraged by extensive use of a battery of governmental assistance devices, many of which involved financing which was exempted from the *encadrements* and some of which involved money creation. An important example of this export promotion program is the collection of policies and arrangements with two groups of African countries with which

TABLE 28

French Foreign Exchange Reserves and Related Assets
(In $US millions)

| Asset | 1974 | 1975 | 1976 | 1977 | 1978 | 1979 | 1980 |
|---|---|---|---|---|---|---|---|
| Foreign Exchange Holdings | 3,753 | 7,442 | 4,377 | 4,694 | 8,305 | 16,100 | 25,338 |
| Special Drawing Rights (SDRs) | 248 | 286 | 263 | 284 | 373 | 849 | 935 |
| IMF Reserve Position | 525 | 729 | 979 | 895 | 600 | 630 | 1,067 |
| Total Reserves Minus Gold | 4,526 | 8,457 | 5,619 | 5,873 | 9,278 | 17,579 | 27,340 |
| Gold at National Valuation | 4,261 | 14,133 | 12,840 | 16,717 | 22,340 | 34,195 | 49,991 |
| Total All Items | 8,787 | 22,590 | 18,459 | 22,590 | 31,618 | 51,774 | 77,331 |

Source: *International Financial Statistics* (Washington: International Monetary Fund, September 1981), p. 153.

France has for some years maintained special economic relationships: the franc zone countries (Benin, Cameroon, Central African Republic, Chad, Comoro Islands, Congo, Gabon, Ivory Coast, Mali, Niger, Senegal, Togo, and Upper Volta); and five other countries enjoying special trade privileges: Algeria, Morocco, Tunisia, Guinea, and Mauritania (Madagascar, although not among these, has a currency closely tied to the franc). Imports from France by these countries grew much faster than their exports to France; by 1978 these and other African countries accounted for France's largest area balance of trade surplus.[30] Table 29 shows this area distribution data on France's exports and trade balances for selected years, and it also indicates the drain exerted by her balance of trade deficit with the oil-exporting countries, which is the largest of those shown.

More recent and more detailed data on directions of trade are given

TABLE 29

Distribution of France's Export and Trade Balance
for Selected Areas, 1973-78
(Billions of U.S. dollars)

| Regions | Share in Percent of France's Exports | | | Balance of Trade (Surplus or Deficit Amount) | | |
|---|---|---|---|---|---|---|
| | 1973 | 1975 | 1978 | 1973 | 1975 | 1978 |
| Developed Countries | 76.4% | 68.8% | 71.0% | − $1.1 | − $1.5 | − $3.9 |
| Oil Exporting Countries | 4.6 | 8.7 | 7.9 | − 2.0 | − 4.7 | − 5.3 |
| Centrally Planned Countries | 3.5 | 5.5 | 3.5 | 0.2 | 1.1 | 0.2 |
| *Less Developed Country Areas:* | | | | | | |
| Latin America | 3.0 | 3.0 | 2.9 | 0.2 | 0.5 | 0.4 |
| Middle East | 1.6 | 1.9 | 1.9 | 0.4 | 0.7 | 1.0 |
| Asia | 1.9 | 2.5 | 2.5 | − 0.1 | 0.3 | 0.2 |
| Africa | 6.5 | 7.7 | 7.2 | 0.5 | 1.6 | 2.2 |
| Total Dollar Amounts | ... | ... | ... | − $1.0 | − $1.0 | − $2.9 |

*Source:* P. A. Wellons, "African Borrowers and Banks: The Political Economy of International Credit," a paper presented at the Annual Meeting of the International Academy of International Business, New Orleans, La., October 23, 1980, Table 10, p. 18.

*Note:* Percents do not add to 100 because miscellaneous countries, in total less than 3 percent, are not shown in table.

30. P. A. Wellons, "African Borrowers and Banks: The Political Economy of International Credit," a paper presented at the Annual Meeting of the International Academy of International Business, New Orleans, La., October 23, 1980, p. 18. This is quoted by kind permission of the author.

in Table 30. Trade with Africa increased significantly: exports to African nations by the end of 1980 accounted for slightly more than 13 percent of all French exports, in contrast to about 7 percent for 1978 (see Table 29). Table 30, incidentally, also shows that France's dominant trading partner in Europe in 1980 was West Germany, and that imports from Middle Eastern countries (except Israel) were almost three times as large as exports to them.

Trade surpluses vis-à-vis the African nations were promoted vigorously by the Barre government, not merely to expand the export business but also as a means of offsetting the deficits incurred by the excess of imports from OPEC nations over exports to them. The government employed various devices in these efforts, many of which operated through the French banking system. These included exemptions from the *encadrements* for financing export credits to African buyers, subsidized interest rates, government guarantees for

TABLE 30

Directions of French Trade for Selected
Countries and Regions, 1980
(Millions of U.S. dollars)

| | Imports into France | Percent | Exports from France | Percent |
|---|---|---|---|---|
| *Countries* | | | | |
| Belgium-Luxembourg | $   939.4 | 8.36 | $   866.6 | 9.32 |
| Italy | 1,055.5 | 9.39 | 1,159.2 | 12.50 |
| Japan | 230.9 | 2.05 | 91.5 | 0.99 |
| Netherlands | 609.0 | 5.42 | 451.7 | 4.87 |
| Spain | 325.3 | 2.89 | 265.6 | 2.86 |
| Sweden | 172.4 | 1.53 | 120.6 | 1.30 |
| Switzerland | 252.6 | 2.25 | 435.1 | 4.69 |
| U.K. | 607.1 | 5.40 | 646.7 | 6.97 |
| U.S.A. | 894.5 | 7.96 | 410.1 | 4.42 |
| U.S.S.R. | 297.1 | 2.64 | 205.4 | 2.21 |
| West Germany | 1,817.9 | 16.17 | 1,486.4 | 16.02 |
| *Regions* | | | | |
| EEC | $5,202.0 | 46.29% | $4,818.2 | 51.94% |
| Africa | 977.3 | 8.70 | 1,225.6 | 13.21 |
| Far East (except Japan) | 319.3 | 2.84 | 219.2 | 2.36 |
| Middle East | 1,544.5 | 13.74 | 437.5 | 4.72 |
| Total from or to All Countries | $11,237.7 | 100.00 | $9,275.9 | 100.00 |

*Source:* Organization for Economic Cooperation and Development, *Statistics of Foreign Trade, Monthly Bulletin* (Paris: OECD, July 1981), pp. 62–63.

loans to support exports to Africa, and credit arrangements which blended foreign assistance with various commercial credits and which were administered by cadres of French government adminis-trators in residence in African countries. Another important feature of these promotional activities is the nature of the currency arrange-ments between France and the franc zone countries, which serve to minimize exchange risks on franc loans to the latter.[31]

The government also made extensive efforts to finance current account deficits abroad. One method involved promoting the place-ment of long-term bond issues (both French franc Eurobonds and gov-ernment bond issues) in OPEC nations. Another device was the arrangement of various kinds of bilateral credits with clients in the OPEC nations.

When France sells long-term financial instruments to clients in OPEC nations, she can, in essence, transfer part of the impact of pay-ment for current consumption of energy imports to the future dates at which the instruments become due. Immediate, adverse impacts upon the current account are thereby lessened and time is "bought," so to speak, during which short- and medium-term economic devel-opments may take place which would render France better able to pay for the debts at the time they become due. This simplified sce-nario may be highly inaccurate and in any case is not free of prob-lems. Reducing the impact of the oil bill on current consumption, for example, generates a conflict with other government policies, such as that of discouraging current energy use by the various devices dis-cussed earlier. Nevertheless, this time-deferral policy is pursued because having to absorb the full impact of the energy bill in the short term would produce political and economic traumas.

Both the financing and export promotion policies are controversial. One of the problems associated with the former has already been mentioned; with respect to the latter, we have also noted earlier that exemptions to the *encadrements* for the purpose of promoting exports made substantial contributions to money supply growth and to the generation of inflationary pressures on the domestic economy. Promoting exports to less-developed nations in the franc zone and elsewhere in Africa by export credits and other methods is inter-preted by some as a means of transferring part of the burden of French energy-related deficits to these countries, which are regarded as less able to afform them—thereby perpetuating unfortunate mani-festations of colonialism. Still others have reservations concerning the role of France's extensive administrative apparatus in export promo-

31. Wellons, pp. 20–27.

tion and her use of a diverse collection of *dirigiste* weapons in the pursuit of these activities.

## Notes on Chapter 3

On the operation of French financial markets, three sources, in addition to those cited, are useful: *Marchés des capitaux et taux d'intérêt*, by Y. Simon (Paris: Economica, 1975); *Le Système monétaire français*, by A. Coutière (Paris: Economic, 1977); and "Sur les taux d'intérêt en France," by J. M. Grandmont and G. Neel, *Revue économique* 24 (1973):460–72. Brief accounts of French financial markets appear in R. Weston's *Domestic and International Banking: The Effects of Monetary Policy* (London: Croom Helm, 1980) and in D. Lomax and P. Gutmann's *The Euromarkets and International Financial Policies* (New York: John Wiley and Sons, 1981). A good reference on organizational developments in the French banking system and their recent background is H. Fournier's "L'Evolution des banques françaises: les réformes de 1966–1972 et leur conséquences," in *The Development of Financial Institutions in Europe 1956–1976*, edited by J. E. Wadsworth, J. S. G. Wilson, and H. Fournier (Leyden: A. W. Sitjhoff, 1977). An account of monetary policies and the French banking system prior to 1973 is "Monetary Policy in France," by P. Dieterlen and H. Durand, in *Monetary Policy in Twelve Industrial Countries*, edited by K. Holbik (Boston: Federal Reserve Bank of Boston, 1973). Also of interest are the OECD publications *Monetary Policy in France* (Paris: OECD, 1974) and *Monetary Targets and Inflation Control* (Paris: OECD, 1979).

An interesting study of bank regulation in foreign countries is A. Tschoegl's *The Regulation of Foreign Banks: Policy Formation in Countries outside the United States* (New York: Salomon Brothers Center for the Study of Financial Institutions, New York University, 1981). A discussion of French banks can also be found in J. D. Aronson, *Money and Power: Banks and the World Monetary Systems* (Beverly Hills, Cal.: Sage Publications, 1978).

Two illuminating articles, technical in nature, which refer to monetary economics issues in the setting of the French economy are "The Monetary Approach to Official Reserves and the Foreign Exchange Rate in France 1962–74: Some Structural Estimates," by J. Mélitz and H. Sterdyniak, *American Economic Review* 69 (1979):818–31; and "The Impact of Monetary and Fiscal Policies on the French Financial System," by A. Fourçans, *Journal of Monetary Economics* 4 (1978): 519–41.

The *encadrements* system is discussed in M. Chazelas, J. F. Dauvisis, and G. Maarek's "L'Expérience française d'encadrement du crédit," *Banque de France cahiers économiques et monétaires* 6 (1978).

Questions of monetary policy and inflation are now often discussed in terms of the controversy surrounding "monetarism" and its implications for fiscal and other economic policies. An introductory survey of monetarist ideas is W. Poole's *Money and the Economy: A Monetarist View* (Reading, Mass.: Addison-Wesley Publishing Co., 1978). A discussion which touches upon philosophical and economic issues related to money in the modern economic system, and various views towards it, is S. H. Frankel's *Two Philosophies of Money, The Conflict of Trust and Authority* (New York: St. Martin's Press, 1977).

In the discussion presented in the fourth section of Chapter 3 we gave considerable attention to the role of monetary targets in the application of monetary policy. A recent book presents papers expressing various views on monetary targets: *Monetary Targets*, edited by B. Griffiths and G. E. Wood (New York: St. Martin's Press, 1981). Inflation expectations and their impact on actual inflation rates are the subject of rapidly expanding research efforts. A good survey of key issues related to such expectations is "Recent Developments in Monetary Theory," by R. J. Barro and S. Fischer, *Journal of Monetary Economics* 2 (1976):133–67. A paper dealing with expected inflation is D. K. Pierce's "Comparing Survey and Rational Measures of Expected Inflation," *Journal of Money, Credit and Banking* 11 (1979):445–56.

Aspects of the mix of monetary and fiscal policies in the setting of interrelated economies are studied in *Towards Full Employment and Price Stability*, by P. McCracken, G. Carli, H. Giersch, et al. (Paris: OECD, 1977). This study is examined and commented upon in papers by P. Korteweg ("Towards Full Employment and Price Stability: An Assessment and Appraisal of the OECD's McCracken Report" [pp. 131–60]), and by R. E. Lucas (pp. 161–68) and S. Fischer (pp. 169–78), all of which appear in *Policies for Employment, Prices and Exchange Rates*, edited by K. Brunner and A. H. Meltzer (Amsterdam: North-Holland Publishing Co., 1979). Another discussion of inflation, inflation expectations, and stabilization policies involving the mix of fiscal and monetary policies is S. Weintraub's *Our Stagflation Malaise: Ending Inflation and Unemployment* (Westport, Conn.: Quorum Books, 1981). Relationships between monetary policy, the balance of payments, and stabilization policy are examined in H. A. Poniachek's *Monetary Independence under Flexible Exchange Rates* (Lexington, Mass.: Lexington Books, 1979). A comparative study of macroeconomic policies in Western Europe, including France, which attaches central importance to the international transmission of impulses to growth or stagnation and stability or instability, is "Macroeconomic Policies in Western European Countries: 1973-1977," by L. Izzo and L. Spaventa, in *Macroeconomic Policies for Growth and Stability: A European Perspective*, a symposium sponsored by the Institut für Weltwirtschaft an der Universität Kiel, edited by H. Giersch (Tübingen: J. C. B. Mohr, 1979):73-135.

# 4

# Concluding Comments

## The Initial Socialist Program
## and the Continuing Economic Problems

In May 1981 Mitterand won the presidency, and in the following month French voters gave his Socialist party an absolute parliamentary majority. Problems of unemployment, inflation, external equilibrium, and energy use, which the Socialists had successfully managed to associate with Giscard d'Estaing and the center-right coalition in the course of the elections, have become the troublesome inheritance of the new government. What happened throughout the remainder of 1981 as this government addressed the same old problems?

Unemployment, having risen 22 percent in the 12 months from July 1980 through July 1981, continued to rise. Employment continued to grow by only slight amounts, despite the sudden spurt of post-election subsidies aimed at public sector job creation. Price controls were selectively reintroduced, a temporary freeze on prices of services as well as on some basic food items was established, and private enterprises were urged to limit price increases to no more than 8 percent in the ensuing 12-month period.

Inflation continued its upward movement and was expected to average between 14 and 15 percent for the year 1981 – an increase over the high level of 1980. At the same time, inflation rates of France's major European trading partners were declining, thereby creating increasingly adverse inflation differentials between France and these countries in 1981. The money stock (M2) grew at a 17 percent annual rate in the first seven months of the year, a figure which exceeds by a considerable amount the target of 10 percent set by the Barre administration for 1981. It appears that M2 growth for the full year will surpass 14 percent and will also exceed nominal GDP growth for the year.

With respect to external equilibrium and balance of payments problems, the government took quick action to defend the franc within the European Monetary System (EMS), beginning with massive market interventions in the form of expenditures of US$ 6 billion in the month of May (out of total foreign exchange reserves, exclusive of gold, of about US$ 27 billion). By the end of September, France's

cumulative loss in foreign exchange reserves attributable to supporting the franc had risen to more than US$ 9 billion, or more than a
third of the country's foreign exchange holdings other than gold.
Exchange controls were tightened considerably – mainly on French
residents – and border surveillance was increased. Domestic interest
rates rose sharply after the election and remained at high levels until
October, when they softened somewhat following the EMS currency
realignments agreed upon the early part of that month (day-to-day
money market rates averaged nearly 20 percent in June, in contrast to
a March average of 11.72 percent, and were 17.09 percent for
October – still relatively high).[1] The government was ostensibly using
high interest rates in an attempt to attract capital into France; but
these interest rates, as well as rising wage rates, also exerted downward influences upon domestic investment, although the government
attempted to blunt some of the consequences of this policy by grant-
ing concessional interest rates to some domestic producers. Private
investment, which had stagnated even under the market-oriented
encouragements of the Barre program, appeared to become even
more sluggish after the elections, declining by 14 percent in 1981,
according to one estimate.

The October currency realignment devalued the franc by 3 percent
against the currencies of Belgium, Denmark, and Ireland, while the
West German mark and Dutch guilder were raised in value by 5½
percent. Despite the government's vigorous efforts relating to foreign
exchange matters, however, the franc remained weak and France's
current account deficit continued to grow.

The minimum wage was raised by 10 percent (3.3 percent would
have been the regular quarterly adjustment), and the government
inaugurated a stimulative fiscal policy. The minimum social pension
was increased by 20 percent, and social security benefits to families
with two or more children were raised 25 percent. It was intended
that the cost of these measures be partially covered by a surtax on
high incomes, by additional taxes on banks and oil companies, and by
an increase in the value-added tax on selected luxury items. Also, in
an attempt to offset partially the increased cost to employers
produced by the rise in the minimum wage, social security taxes on
them were reduced for relatively low-paid employees (those whose
total earnings are less than 120 percent of the minimum wage).

These and other increases in government expenditures caused the
budget deficit to grow significantly. A government estimate as of the
end of September placed the deficit for 1981 between 70 and 75 bil-

1. *World Financial Markets* (New York: Morgan Guaranty Trust Co., November 1981),
p. 16.

lion francs, an increase of about 40 percent over 1980. This deficit would be about 2.8 percent of nominal GDP, a higher percentage than for any year since 1976 and surpassing even that for 1975, a particularly bad year for fiscal performance (see Chapter 1).

The government also announced a nationalization plan targeting some industrial sectors and placing the entire banking system under government control (this plan was recently approved by the courts). A feature of the Socialist election platform had been a reduction in the growth of France's nuclear generating capacity and a cutting back on other goals of the existing policy. Shortly after the election, government spokespersons announced that rollbacks in energy policy of the kind advocated during the election would be enacted. By the fall of the year, however, the government had had second thoughts on the energy issue and retreated to a position which, apart from the embellishments of the announced rhetoric, appeared to be close to that developed under the Barre administration. Fears relating to the problem of unemployment were cited by the government as the major reason for the turnabout.

As of the end of 1981, France was the only major EEC nation currently employing stimulative monetary and fiscal policies. West Germany's Bundesbank has been following a policy of monetary restraint for some months now; Chancellor Schmidt has reiterated his determination to hold down government spending, and the government is committed to reduce the budget deficit from the 38 billion marks estimated for 1981 to about 26 billion marks in 1982. Inflation rates are expected to decline in the Netherlands, in Denmark (there has been some reduction in real wages in both these countries), and in the United Kingdom. Italy, another major trading partner of France, although not intending to follow stimulative economic policies, will continue to have difficulties in curbing inflation and moderating budget deficits; nevertheless, it is expected to make some progress in reducing its current account deficit in 1982.

## A Look Ahead

The prospects for the medium term (two to four years into the future) appear to be cloudy, and most professional forecasters and analysts are avoiding, when they can, the announcement of numerical forecasts. The unemployment problem is likely to continue worsening. INSEE forecasts made in 1979 called for high rates of unemployment until at least 1983, and under additional reasonable assumptions until 1985. (It must be said that econometric forecasts of unemployment for more than one and a half years into the future, in

France and elsewhere, have been relatively poor.) Measures taken so far to stimulate employment appear to be increasing labor costs, and the status of productivity gains is highly uncertain.[2] The "share the work" proposals of the government, which have the strong support of the labor unions and the left wing of the Socialist party, apparently do not contain arrangements for a proportional reduction in wages or even for the maintenance of existing wage levels in the course of work reductions, and thus offer the prospect of further additions to labor costs. Private investment, in the face of all these problems as well as government pressures to restrain increases in output prices and selective reintroduction of price controls, is likely to continue stagnating, and prospects for restoring real economic growth even to moderate levels are poor.

The softening of oil demand on the part of Western nations, related to the energy-saving efforts spurred by high oil prices and recession conditions in these countries, has benefitted France by moderating energy-related import costs, but medium-term prospects are for continued large expenditures on imported oil and coal. There remains a great deal of uncertainty in future energy supplies. Despite the ambitious French program for creating domestic energy sources—which we have noted will be continued by the Socialist government—energy imports will be a costly burden for years to come.

In addition, the temporary benefits of the selective devaluations arranged through the EMS are likely to be offset by the increasingly unfavorable inflation differentials vis-à-vis France's major trading partners for the medium term. These forces, together with continuing pressures exerted by energy imports and the fact that any further improvement in France's international competitiveness is unlikely, suggest that current account deficits will continue to be troublesome and that the franc will experience heavy weather for some time.

It is likely that fiscal policy will become even more stimulative, at least over the next two years. We have noted that the budget deficit for 1981 was estimated to be between 70 and 75 billion francs. For the year 1982 the government recently projected an increase in total expenditures of about 28 percent over 1981, an increase in total revenues of about 19 percent, and a deficit of 95.4 billion francs.[3] Deficits projected by the government usually err on the side of underestimation; alternate estimates of the 1982 deficit are in excess of 100 billion francs, and some are in the interval from 130 to 140 billion

2. Labor unions have indicated some willingness to consider zero real wage changes, on the average, provided lower-wage workers receive "some" improvement; but what this may mean in terms of wage costs is unknown.
3. *L'Economie* October 5, 1981, p. 13.

francs. It seems reasonable to believe that the deficit for 1982 will be more than 50 percent larger than that for 1981 – possibly even twice that year's level – and that it is highly likely the deficit will exceed 3 percent of GDP.

The use of stimulative fiscal and monetary policies can be seriously questioned, particularly when it is recalled that these policies were initiated from a base of slightly more than 13 percent inflation. The government is attempting to reflate the economy when the economy is already experiencing a high rate of inflation. Inflation has been the "running sore" of French economic policy for more than 30 years and it is unlikely that further increases in inflation can be used to trade off against reductions in unemployment, even if other disadvantages of rising inflation can be accepted. There is a very real danger that these policies will generate both increased inflation and increased unemployment in the medium term. Moreover, there may be no trade-off between them for policymakers to exploit. In any case, such stimulative policies, following more than five years of increasing inflation and stagnating investment growth, can be expected to exacerbate adverse inflation expections. They may produce some short-run improvements, but these benefits are likely to be exhausted within the new government's first year.

Developments in the relationships between unemployment and inflation in France since 1965 offer considerable support for these observations. Figure 10, in which each point is labelled by the corresponding year, gives a plot of annual CPI inflation and unemployment rates since 1965. The standard downward-sloping Phillips curve of introductory textbooks does not summarize or "fit" this set of data. Only in the subperiod 1974 through 1978 (overlapping the years of the Barre program but not coextensive with it) is a downward-sloping curve suggested. (In other words, only in this subperiod, consisting of four observations, is it suggested that lower rates of inflation may be associated with higher unemployment rates.) For the remaining years shown, inflation rates and unemployment rates rise together.

Economists have found it necessary to extend Phillips curve analyses to take account of influences that were omitted from the original formulation. Some have suggested that the relationship between inflation and unemployment is influenced by lagged effects; others take the view that the relationship shifts with time, producing "layers" of Phillips curves which describe trade-offs between inflation and unemployment but at successively higher levels for both. Still others stress the importance of expectations concerning inflation on the part of economic agents and attempt to include an expectations variable in the relationship (the expectations-augmented Phillips anal-

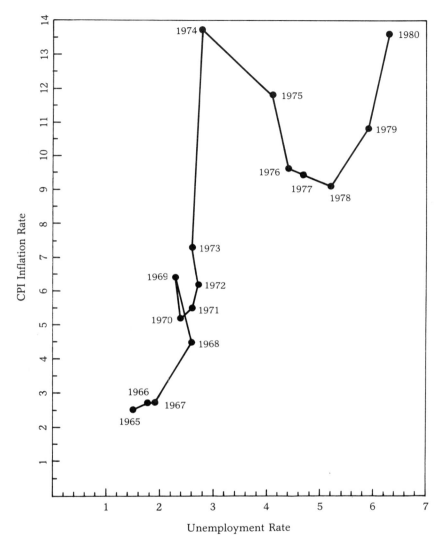

**Figure 10.**     **Annual CPI Inflation and Unemployment Rates
in France, 1965–80**

ysis). A refinement of this extension is the inclusion of yet another
term which describes how expectations are formed. This term is
usually modelled adaptively (the Phillips analysis with adaptive
expectations).

Still another school of thought has advanced the natural rate hypothesis, which states that there is no permanent trade-off between inflation and unemployment. In this view, real economic magnitudes tend to be independent of nominal magnitudes, at least in a long-run equilibrium sense. Trade-offs can exist in the short run, but these are regarded as necessarily transitory; they stem largely from unexpected inflation and disappear when expectations adjust to inflationary experience. In the long run, inflationary surprises are assimilated, expectations are modified, and unemployment attains a natural or equilibrium rate. These conditions imply that in the long run the Phillips curve is a vertical line which intersects the unemployment rate axis at a point (or number) which is the natural rate.[4]

These issues are the subject of much research and debate, and little testing of these theories using French data is known to the writer. Further discussion is beyond the scope of this study but two observations concerning the data in Figure 10 are tentatively offered. First, these data appear on the surface to be consistent with a natural rate approach; a vertical straight line seems to offer a fairly good visual fit to the data. Second, it seems reasonable that unemployment rates should lag inflation rates, whatever the expectations issue may be. Figure 11 shows a plot of CPI inflation rates against unemployment rates lagged one year (for example, the first point at the lower left portion of the figure is the 1966 inflation rate and the 1965 unemployment rate; the point at the extreme upper right is the 1980 inflation rate and the 1979 unemployment rate). Figure 11 is similar to Figure 10 in that it displays a conventional trade-off only for the subperiod 1974 to 1978. Thus, introducing a lag of one year in unemployment leaves the general "shape" of the relationship largely unaltered. Stated another way, inflation and unemployment rates lagged one year also appear, by and large, to rise together through time.

We have given a somber *prévision* of the effects of the Mitterand policies in the medium term. These policies abandoned the restrained approach of the Barre program, returned to the demand stimulation motif typical of Western nations in the 1960s, shifted the focus from the medium term toward the short run, and greatly extended the gov-

4. Various refinements of Phillips curve analyses are discussed in H. Frisch, "Inflation Theory 1963–1975: A Second Generation Survey," *Journal of Economic Literature* 15 (1977):1290–302; R. J. Gordon, "Recent Developments in the Theory of Inflation and Unemployment," *Journal of Monetary Economics* 2 (1976):185–219; D. Laidler, "Expectations and the Phillips Trade Off: A Commentary," *Scottish Journal of Political Economy* 23 (1976):55–72; and M. Friedman, *Unemployment versus Inflation: An Evaluation of the Phillips Curve*, IEA Occasional Paper No. 44 (London: The Institute of Economic Affairs, 1976). The adaptive expectations version of Phillips curves takes one into the rational expectations literature, a good survey of which is B. T. McCallum's "Rational Expectations and Macroeconomic Stabilization Policy: An Overview," *Journal of Money, Credit and Banking* 12 (1980):716–46.

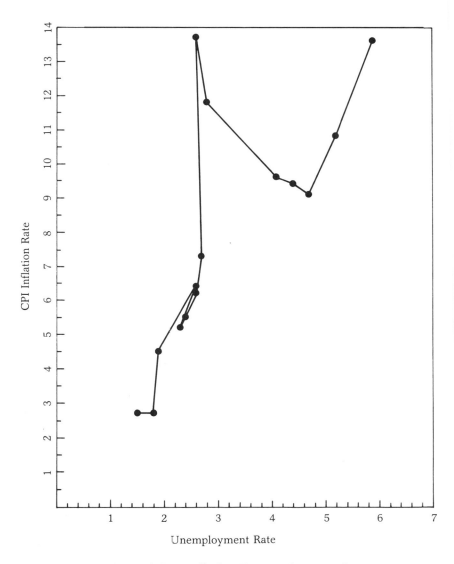

**Figure 11.    Annual CPI Inflation Rate and Unemployment Rate
Lagged One Year in France, 1965–80**

ernment's administrative control over economic organization. This
was done, moreover, at a time when many other Western nations
were moving away from demand-driven policies emphasizing short-
run effects and towards a more surgical application of policy instru-

ments chosen with a view towards other than short-run considerations. The Mitterand policies may turn out to be successful, but it appears doubtful to the writer for the reasons stated earlier. It is unlikely that the Socialist program, if it continues on its present course, will have done as well by the time of the next parliamentary election in 1986 as the Barre program did during the period 1976–81 – whatever were the shortcomings of the latter.